EVERYDAY
RACISM

EVERYDAY RACISM

A Book for All Americans

ANNIE S. BARNES

SOURCEBOOKS, INC.®
NAPERVILLE, ILLINOIS

Published by Sourcebooks, Inc.
P.O. Box 4410, Naperville, Illinois 60567-4410
(630) 961-3900
FAX: (630)961-2168

First edition published 2000 by The Pilgrim Press. Paperback edition published 2000 by
Sourcebooks, Inc., by arrangement with The Pilgrim Press.

Library of Congress Cataloging-in-Publication Data
Barnes, Annie S.
    Everyday racism: A Book for All Americans / Annie S. Barnes.
    p. cm.
    ISBN 1-57071-653-6 (alk. paper)
    1. Afro-Americans—Social conditions—1975-2. Race discrimination—United States. 3.
        Racism—United States—Psychological aspects. 4. Interpersonal relations—United
        States. 5. United States—Race relations. 6. Afro-Americans—Interviews. I. Title.

E185.86 .B3735 2000
305.896'073—dc21

00-044036

Printed and bound in the United States of America
DR   10   9   8   7   6   5   4   3   2   1

CONTENTS

INTRODUCTION

I'M BLACK AND
I'M PROUD

S ay it loud," James Brown sang in 1968, "I'm black, and I'm proud." During the civil rights era, African Americans did take pride in James Brown's message, in the harsh demand for justice of Malcolm X and other black leaders, and in the inspiring and prophetic words of Martin Luther King Jr. In the late 1990s many believe that the need for such affirmations has long since faded. Yet the stories compiled in this book about the hostility and resentment that many blacks experience at the hands of white people demonstrate how much we still need to say—and say it loud—"We're black and we're proud."

WHY I WROTE THIS BOOK

In my quest to learn more about young African Americans, I conducted a series of interviews at Norfolk State University in Norfolk, Virginia, where I taught anthropology and sociology for twenty-five years. The students in my Social Science Research Skills Seminar were my research team. Dr. Thelma Thompson, vice president for academic affairs at Norfolk State, provided assistance and encouragement.

My research team and I asked 146 students at Norfolk State to detail one or more of their three worst racist experiences in all parts of the country. When an experience did not occur in their home state, they said so.

Using fictitious names, I share the experiences of those black college students, men and women, between the ages of eighteen and forty. Most were born in the last twenty-five years, so, in general, segregation has not been part of their experience. Racism has. By racism, I am referring to a kind of "superiority virus" carried by whites and demonstrated in their body language, speech, blatant and subtle actions, isolating attitude, and subtle retaliation. This virus is meant to cure another virus—personal insecurity—that damages the lives of blacks of all ages everywhere, emotionally and physically. Not all whites practice racism. Some are secure and have respect for all people. Some feel inadequate but know it's unfair to hurt blacks to make up for their own shortcomings. Others try to make themselves feel significant by practicing racism whenever they encounter black people.

I had seven specific motivations for writing this book. First, I hope to develop among white Americans an increased awareness of racism and its harmful effects on black Americans. Second, I hope to promote and help develop better relations between blacks and whites. I do not believe that white Americans comprehend the extent to which racism impinges upon the everyday lives of blacks. It is my hope that the candid, firsthand reports of young black men and women, analyzed in light of current literature on racism in America and of personal experience, will help provide a model for building a solid base for improved relations among all races. Ultimately, my goal is to urge whites to think highly enough of themselves that they are not compelled to practice racism—an immoral behavior.

Third, I want to trouble the scholarly waters about racism. Previous books—I have in mind those by Oscar Lewis and William Julius Wilson—have focused solely on poor blacks' experiences of racism.[1] These books are important; the experiences described are real and cannot be denied. Yet my problem with these studies is that they do little to distinguish bad treatment prompted by class from that prompted by race. This book, in contrast, focuses on middle-class, working-class, and poor blacks, because their experiences demonstrate how pervasive racist attitudes are among whites—even about blacks of a similar socioeconomic status. Some of the students I interviewed, although from working-class and poor backgrounds, found the means to attend college. These students prove that poverty is not necessarily self-perpetuating. Racism, as their experiences indicate, is at least as much a handicap to their success as economic disadvantage. Middle-class students document a similar handicap. Ostensibly, they have everything they need to function in the white world—money, upbringing, education. Yet they are stymied in their quest to live full, productive lives by the racism they encounter at every turn.

Other scholarly books, especially *Discrimination American Style: Institutional Racism and Sexism* by Joe R. Feagin and Clairece Booher Feagin, focus on the settings in which racism occurs. They omit discussions of the hurt in blacks' hearts that comes from seemingly automated racism in whites, any analytical interpretation of racism, and suggestions for countering racism.[2] Scholars have overlooked the most important aspects of racism—its effect on black people and how to eradicate it. This book closes those gaps. For the first time, laypeople, scholars, and students are provided with a comprehensive picture of American racism.

The fourth reason for writing this book is to clarify that other works, particularly Gunnar Myrdal's often-cited 1944 and 1996 editions of his book *An American Dilemma*, offer interpretations that are only partially correct. Myrdal, a Swedish social economist, held that "the American Negro problem is a problem in the heart of the American. It is there that the interracial tension has its focus. It is there that the decisive struggle goes on."[3] Yet my findings contradict Myrdal's assessment. I believe that this "interracial tension" or "decisive struggle" is not shared by whites and blacks and that the vast majority of white Americans do not struggle with how they treat blacks or with how blacks are treated by others. With this book, I hope to stir up some angst in the hearts of white Americans. More whites need to feel conflicted about racism. Many need to see the contradiction between their Christian precepts and their behavior toward people of another race. They need to confess how they use these precepts to justify their racism. And they need to stop practicing racism. I believe that Myrdal gives whites too much credit by stating that white Americans struggle with racism and too little by maintaining that the problems of racism will be resolved as a result of this struggle.

Fifth, I mean to describe, analyze, and interpret the reality of modern racism. In this book, people describe their real-life struggles, often in stark terms. The usual strategy that authors adopt in books about racism is to silence the voices of the victims, neglect describing their feelings, ignore their conclusions, and avoid remedies, perhaps even to defend those whites who do not engage in racist acts. Some might go so far as to congratulate these whites and shift the focus to a bigoted few. This strategy fails because it permits the majority of whites—those who do not think of themselves as bigots—to be satisfied with their inactivity. That is not my intention here. In *Everyday Racism*, I hope to make it clear that when whites do not actively work to eliminate racism, they remain part of the problem. I believe it is essential for these voices to be heard, for only when we are willing to listen to the powerful, undiluted pain of those who face racism every day can we begin a dialogue with real meaning and real promise.

A sixth reason for writing this book is to specifically describe the effects of racism. Racism hurts blacks' feelings, damages their self-esteem, makes them physically and emotionally ill, robs them of economic opportunities, and causes them to feel inferior to whites. Racism discourages some blacks from trying to succeed and causes them to feel like failures. Not all blacks respond this way—many respond to white people's negative behavior by feeling equal or superior. Some use racism for their own good; they fight it by becoming successful. Racism creates rifts in communities and in society that are carried from generation to generation and that can be so easily repaired. Most blacks yearn for united communities and a united society. Whites are warmly invited to assume the same noble stance. It will not hurt them. Rather, it will engender healthy race relations—and the racist virus will be wiped out forever.

Finally, this work, unlike all the other valuable research, is written to give an insider's view of black-white relations. Growing up as a sharecropper's daughter, experiencing segregation as a young woman, and living in the post–civil rights era have left me well prepared to record the events and to formulate the analyses that comprise this book. I am no stranger to racism. I have had a personal acquaintance with it, from when I was carried in my mother's womb out to the fields of a white racist sharecropper's farm, to the present. I have become mentally and physically ill from racist experiences here, there, and everywhere. One kept me in mental agony, tears, and prayer for at least two weeks. I was hurt. I found it hard to understand how one person could treat another that way. Needless to say, two weeks of suffering interfered with everything I had to do.

Finally, my training in social anthropology, extensive research with blacks and some whites, and constant interaction with white people for almost thirty years—including sharing an apartment building on the beautiful Hague River in Norfolk for seven years, complete with swimming pool, and belonging to a white church for twenty-five years—helped attune me to the types of racism addressed in this book. My experience is not localized. I have tested what is in this book from the North to the South and from the East to the West. Foremost, I learned from blacks with whom I was equally intimate the damages racism creates all over America.

HOW THIS BOOK IS ORGANIZED

In each chapter I concentrate on a specific type of racism encountered by the students I interviewed. The bulk of the chapters consists of the words of these students as they recounted what happened to them in their neighborhoods, at school, at their jobs, while driving down the street, in the swimming pool. I offer only occasional commentary as the stories are narrated, so that these young people can describe their own experiences without the filter of another person's interpretation. Each chapter closes with a section entitled "What to Do About It." In these sections, which I have broken down into subsections entitled "What White People Can Do" and "What Black People Can Do," I suggest strategies for countering the types of racism addressed in each chapter.

Countering racism—and replacing it with fairness, justice, and true acceptance—is the single most important action needed today. It is also the most crucial step toward ensuring that blacks and other people of color feel like complete human beings and full members of society. To achieve this requires the cooperation of everyone, people of all colors, all backgrounds, all ethnic and cultural groups. It is my hope that this book will provide a model and serve as an inspiration.

1

WHEN IT HAPPENS NEXT DOOR

Many African Americans are choosing to live in upscale neighborhoods side-by-side with white people. Many see the ability to live in these neighborhoods as progress. The reasons for this are self-evident. These neighborhoods simply have more of everything than black neighborhoods. The city furnishes these districts with nicer parks, cleaner streets, better landscaping, more efficient garbage collection, stronger police protection, and better schools. Merchants provide cheaper groceries and better merchandise.

Blacks have earned the right to live among whites and to enjoy the good life. Because this country was developed by using free black labor, blacks have paid for the right to live any place they choose—including predominantly white neighborhoods.[1] Blacks, the most discriminated against and exploited immigrants in the Western world, have made life comfortable for whites, been subservient to whites, increased white people's sense of superiority, and helped to develop a country that has made white people wealthy.[2]

Many people think that the days of crude discrimination and bigotry are long gone—that blacks should get over their anger about slavery and move on. After all, blacks are no longer forced to drink from separate drinking fountains or to stand at the back of the bus. Yet the sad truth is that many white people still make it clear that they think of blacks as inferior. Although the stories about racism in these chapters, told by the young black college students I interviewed, are not the most sensational, they are typical of young black people's daily lives and no less descriptive of the terror experienced by these young people who encounter racism day in and day out than the worst horror story.

When I was interviewing students at Norfolk State University, I always started off by asking them about their three worst experiences with racism. Often they responded to this question with stories of being mistreated by white adults and their children in their own neighborhoods—a particularly painful experience to blacks who have striven to be able to live where they want and who want nothing more than to make nice homes where they can feel comfortable.

NOT IN MY BACKYARD

Tragically, many whites, even today, do not want blacks living in their neighborhoods, and certainly not next door. Daniel, a twenty-two-year-old resident of Georgia, recounted this story about being mistreated by neighbors in his apartment complex. Daniel owned a personal radio with earphones that he used to carry around with him as he walked about the building. The supervisor of the complex, who was white, told Daniel that he could no longer listen to his radio in the hallways or on the grounds of the building because it was distracting to his neighbors. But Daniel observed that a white youth in his complex had a similar radio with earphones and that the supervisor never complained about him and let him use it wherever he wanted. Daniel told me, "That hurt me. This nation needs to talk, preach, and practice equality between the races."

Janie, twenty-seven years old and from Michigan, recalled this experience at her apartment building pool:

When I was twenty-three years old, while on summer vacation, my twelve-year-old sister and her black twelve-year-old girlfriend were in our apartment complex pool. They were playing with a five-year-old white girl who asked my sister to blow up an inflatable raft for her. When the little girl's mother saw my sister blowing up the raft, she spanked her daughter and told her, "Never let a nigger put their mouth on anything that belongs to you." Then she ordered the child to stay out of the pool until my sister and her friend had left. They immediately got out of the pool and told me what had happened.

Since I'm my sister's legal guardian, instead of ignoring the experience, I felt that I should talk with the girl's mother. When I asked her what had happened, she became hostile and rude. I stopped arguing with her and instead filed a complaint with the rental office. I'm not sure what happened. Two weeks later, that woman moved out of the apartment complex. Because my sister and friend were subjected to harsh and unfair words, I was angry. I told them that there are a lot of ignorant people in the world and they needed to learn how to handle themselves in racist situations.

Even getting into a neighborhood in the first place can prove difficult for many blacks, including young black students seeking apartments in college towns. Louis, a twenty-three-year-old student from New Jersey, for example, had just finished summer school at Norfolk State University and was staying with a friend in town. He wanted to find his own apartment for the school year. He found a couple of good deals, but none of them panned out. Then he came upon a large colonial house with eight bedrooms occupied by two elderly white women. The rent was low, even for a college town, and included the use of a bedroom, kitchen, and bathroom as well as utilities and cable television.

Louis put on what he called his "white" voice (that is, he spoke like whites who speak very clearly) and told the two landlords about his qualifications, his grade-point average, the jobs he had held, and his parents' jobs. The women said they would be happy to rent to him and asked him to come have a look at the place. When he arrived at the house, however, the landladies changed their tune. They told him that the place had been rented by another man with remarkably similar qualifications. When Louis told them he was the person who had called, they told him he was lying, because the person who had called was white. "What a shame," Louis said. "Did you know that whites can be so easily fooled by blacks?" He told them, "To hell with this house; I'm going to report you to EEOC." That's when the women did an about-face. One of them said, "We'll lower the rent, and you don't have to pay the first month's rent until next month." Louis told them, "No, thank you."

Because black students, particularly males, have difficulty finding good housing, they often need to resort to various techniques, like the one Louis used, to get a foot in the door. Douglas, who is thirty-nine, a Virginia resident, and married to a white woman, told me about the approach he used to find a house to rent. When he found a house he was interested in, he was referred by management to the owner, whom he telephoned. The owner told Douglas that the house had been rented. Doug's wife immediately called back and was told by the same owner that the house was available. The couple then went to see it. When Douglas confronted the owner, she said there had just been a misunderstanding. Douglas told me, "I felt that I had been lied to and that I had gone through a screening process. I was very angry. Needless to say, we got the house." The owner was afraid of being sued.

Sadly, since many black students don't have a white helpmate, they often end up without desirable living quarters. Walter, an eighteen-year-old student from Delaware, talked about apartment hunting in Virginia with three of his friends. They found an attractive apartment complex and entered the business office. A white female manager came only halfway out of her office to acknowledge them, remaining in the doorway. When they told her they were looking for an apartment, she interrupted, "Who is the apartment for?" One of Walter's friends informed her that it was for them. She asked, "Do all of you make at least $17,000 per year?" The friend said that the apartment would be in his mother's name. The manager's response was, "We don't do that." When Walter's friend offered her the money up front, she answered, "We don't do that, either." At that point, the young men realized that they were the victims of outright discrimination, and they quietly left. They did not tell the manager off, because they did not want to lower themselves to her level.

CURTAILED FRIENDSHIPS

Friendships between blacks and whites prepare people of all age groups for a better life. While blacks were doing back-breaking labor to build this country, whites were learning. It is not only fair, it is also morally right for whites to be friendly and teach blacks what they know. It should be kept in mind that blacks gave whites the opportunity to get a head start in learning. If they had shared equal chances at work and learning in classrooms, black and white friendships would be rich and enjoyable, but not imperative.

Friendship between blacks and whites enables both races to feel good about themselves—an achievement that proves their fine humanity—to experience warmth and love, and to enjoy interesting conversation. Friendship between blacks and whites helps people of both races to outgrow their personal insecurities. Before I married, for some summers I worked at the Sleighton Farm School for girls, in Media, Pennsylvania. I became friends with a young Jewish woman about my age. I have never been happier before or since with a friendship. She and I used to visit her home in a wealthy Philadelphia suburb on weekends. Her father mixed wonderful alcoholic drinks. Neither of us drank, but we liked to taste, and her father loved that. Tasting meant that she drank out of the same glass after me—never before—in the presence of her parents.

Our activities—work or play—were always embellished with fresh and inviting conversation. We were friends.

Sadly, many of the students I interviewed reported the grave difficulties they experienced with establishing or maintaining friendships with white people. Many of them experienced racism even more scarring than the sort Douglas and his wife encountered. These experiences were with children in their neighborhoods, often of the same age. It hurts when a white child practices racism just as much as it does when white adults practice it. White children learn from what they see and hear in their families, where some of the ugliest behaviors in America are handed down. If racism among adults were eliminated, then nearly all racist acts in America would be halted.

Hilma, twenty-one and a resident of North Carolina, talked about a neighbor who had taught racist attitudes to a friend who was his daughter.

When I was nineteen I went next door to see my girlfriend Millie, who was white and had been my friend for five years. One evening, Millie's father had a talk with me. He told me that he felt that I wasn't good enough to hang out with Millie, that I had a bad influence on her. He didn't say that because of my behavior. He said it because of the color of my skin. If I had been white, I would have continued as Millie's best friend and as a good neighbor. Millie's father felt that blacks were trying to do better than white people. He said, "Blacks are showoffs and try to outdo whites." Unlike him, my parents had the finer things of life, including nice cars and a beautiful house. Lots of white people hate with a passion seeing blacks do well without selling drugs. They also hate seeing blacks receive an education that no white man or woman can take from them.

What's so sad about Hilma's story is that although it was Millie's father who had a problem with his black neighbors being more successful than he was, it was his daughter and her friend who were made to suffer for it. Millie did not have a problem being friends with Hilma, but because of her father's racism, the friendship was forced to end. She learned firsthand, from her father, a racist's attitude toward blacks.

In Millie's case, it was due to her father's racism, not hers, that a lovely friendship was forced to end. Sometimes white adults are so efficient at teaching racism that their children start to practice it as well as their parents. Mamie, thirty-one, described this experience:

> I was nine years old, and my father was in the military. We lived in a predominantly white neighborhood in North Carolina. Two white families lived behind us. Their parents would not let their children, ages nine and sixteen, play with my brother and me. Their mothers told the children that we had tails and that we had roaches in our homes. Consequently, the children would yell from their back porch, "Look at those nigger tails who live with cockroaches." Then they would throw rocks at us. This child racism ended when my father learned about it. Because he had a higher military rank than their fathers, he "pulled rank" and reprimanded their fathers in his office. When this occurred, the children stopped calling us names, but we never played with them.

What Mamie experienced was the old racist practice of parents warning their daughters that black boys have tails.[3] These modern-day mothers were giving their children a negative perspective of blacks, and the children, sadly, were complying with this teaching.

Some students told me stories about seeking friendship with white children, who though they had not yet been coached in racist stereotypes, engaged in name-calling. Sonya, twenty, had this experience:

> One afternoon, about five years ago, in Virginia Beach, Virginia, I was visiting my boyfriend. When I arrived at his

apartment complex, three young boys were in the parking lot. The boys were between six and eight years of age. Two were white, and one was a light-skinned black. The two white boys were teasing the black boy mercilessly. They called him names, asked him whether or not he was a black person, and similar questions. The little boy was almost in tears. When I saw what was occurring, I decided to intervene. I knew the boy who was being picked on personally, and I wanted to make sure that he was okay. When I asked him if he was alright, one of the white boys told me to mind my own business and called me a nigger. I was shocked to hear a young child be so racist. I tried to ignore the remark; however, the white boys continued to tease the black boy.

A while later, I approached one of the white mothers and told her that her son had called me a nigger and had made hurtful statements to the little black boy. The mother explained that her son had migrated from a country where he had never seen a black person. One of the boys later told me that he was sorry about calling me a name. He also said that he regretted hurting the little black boy's feelings. According to him, he had learned the word *nigger* in a day-care center and in his elementary school.

The young black boy endured racist remarks only because he wanted to play with the white boys—that was his only crime. Although many children do not even understand what the word *nigger* means, like the white children in Sonya's story, others have learned to connect it with what they think of as the inferiority of their playmates. Julie, thirty, gave this example:

My worst experience was in 1976, when I moved into a predominantly white neighborhood in Teaneck, New Jersey. I was about seven years old. Since I was new in the area, I didn't have any playmates. After a week, I began playing with the girl next door, who was about my age. After two weeks of fun and play, Becky's mother came outside and pulled her in the house, saying, "You can't play with that nigger child anymore. She's not good enough for you." Then she turned to me and said, "Get off our property." I went home and told my mother. She told me to never go to my friend's house again. Fortunately, I overcame the situation quickly because I didn't really know what was happening and because another white girl moved in across the street. We played together as if nothing had happened. I was really too young to understand racism.

Though it can often be difficult, as we have seen from the above stories, finding the right white friends is important. Even when black youths have accomplished this, they sometimes still experience prejudice and discrimination. Eighteen-year-old Richard, for example, grew up as a military officer's son on a base in Virginia. He found himself in an even greater minority than the average black child because there were so few black officers on the base. He had a few black friends, but his best friend was a white youth named Pat. Richard and Pat played together all the time and were partners in basketball.

One evening, the boys were playing against an all-white team of boys with whom they sometimes hung out. They beat this team, laughing over their victory. Before Richard knew it, one of the kids from the other team had spit in his hair. Pat started fighting the boy, while Richard kicked him twice. The youth who had spat on Richard ran home and told his mother, who came over and told Pat never to touch her child again. Then she turned to Richard and said, "You look here, nigger, you had better go home and never come around my son again." She didn't call Pat any names, even though he had started the fight.

Richard felt defenseless in the face of such blatant mistreatment and was glad to have his sister defend him. Richard and his sister experienced enormous conflict. Though she had been able to rise to the occasion, she found herself repeating the incident to friends like a well-worn tape. That's the way racism makes blacks act; it hurts, it's frustrating, and it's hard to forget.

Shontell, a twenty-five-year-old mother in Virginia, heard an innocent young white girl tell her daughter that dogs are racists too:

> The worst racist experience that I've had was actually experienced by my daughter, who was six at the time. A white girl her age said to her, "My dog doesn't like black people."

An innocent little white girl had practiced racism. Most likely she had learned it from her parents. Shontell's daughter was too young to fight back. Some black parents attempt to teach their children to handle racism by responding gently and encouraging the perpetrators to consider their actions. As so many know, blacks view racism as the most wicked and immoral behavior in America. This causes some parents to actually teach their children to fully confront racists—ending up in shrunken self-concepts, hurt, arguments, and sometimes fights.

Most black parents don't teach their children how to respond to racist acts and words. When their children are caught off guard, their hurt is deeper.

Though racism can occur anywhere and anytime, blacks are still never prepared for it. Some black parents try to prepare their children—as good parents should—but they simply can't adequately prepare themselves or their children. Racist behavior (the white virus) strikes suddenly and unexpectedly, like a sharp bolt of lightning. There simply isn't time to prepare. The result is a damaged black person—or perhaps a damaged black group.

NEIGHBORHOOD HATE CRIMES

Teaching innocent children to be racists is only one of the more heinous forms of bigotry practiced by adults. The students also described other ways white adults used to indicate their feelings about sharing their neighborhoods with blacks, acts which have now come to be called "hate crimes." Eighteen years after the passage of the Civil Rights Act in 1964, Karl, a twenty-three-year-old student from North Carolina, recounted this story. He was ten years old when it happened. He and his family had just moved and had not been in their house long when Karl realized that they were living in what had formerly been an all-white neighborhood. The only other black family in the neighborhood lived across the street. Karl's family had desired to live in a nicer neighborhood, the type of neighborhood where whites usually live, and they had taken the risk that it might be unfriendly. One morning, they awakened to find their mailbox chopped down and the words "Niggers, go home" spray painted on their driveway. White adults, not their children, had been responsible for this racist prank.

Although only a youth, Karl became angry. He cooled down later, figuring that it was an isolated case. His father, in contrast, took it as the first salvo in a neighborhood war. He swore that he would defend his family—and get even. During the next week, he sat in the shrubbery with his gun ready, waiting for the racists to return. Karl said, "It's a good thing that they didn't return because my daddy might have committed homicide and be serving a prison term today." Karl is like many young black adults who bare the brunt of racism internally. His father, on the other hand, had already suffered a lifetime of racism and was ready to fight back.

Some young people related stories of receiving terrifying threats. Roger, who was nineteen when I interviewed him, had his worst encounter with racism in Columbia, South Carolina, when he was fourteen years old. He and one of his white friends were riding their bicycles to a store in their integrated neighborhood. They heard a white man yell from his house, "The KKK is here to stay." Roger was frightened because he knew that the Ku Klux Klan was a frightening and dangerous reality for blacks in the South.

Wayne, eighteen and from Virginia, also found that some white adults do not believe that blacks should be living next door and had some very menacing ways of expressing this. When he was ten years old, Wayne and a friend were walking down the street to the nearby basketball courts. To get there, they had to pass by a house where six white males were sitting on the porch drinking beer. When they saw Wayne and his friend, one of them asked, "What are you niggers doing around here?" He looked at the other men and said, "Get the gun." Wayne and his friend ran away as fast as they could.

It is shocking how often white racists use the word *nigger* to express disdain and a sense of superiority. These men also gave Wayne and his friend a lesson in violence. When you don't like somebody, just use a gun. Could blacks, especially males, also have internalized this type of violence?

Clearly, as I've shown earlier, whites learn violence from their parents and other adults and use it to mark their territory. Kitty, a thirty-five-year-old from South Carolina, related this classic and terrifying hate crime in her neighborhood:

> One of the worst racist experiences that I have had was when a cross was burned in my friend's front yard. It was burned by white male students. The crossburning was not only directed at my friend but at our entire black neighborhood. The young men burned the cross because blacks in my neighborhood were protesting our high school's mascot, a Confederate soldier. This incident created even more racial animosity at our school.

These young white men had picked up Ku Klux Klan behavior from their parents and other bigoted people in their neighborhood and had learned to enact it when it suited their purposes. It is tragic that white men learn racial hatred so early. Usually their childhood experiences follow them all their lives, and these whites only grow more and more mean-spirited and disrespectful as they get older.

PERSONAL ASSAULTS

As awful as verbal abuse and threats are, physical violence is obviously much worse. Many of the students I interviewed have also been personally assaulted.

Jonathan, twenty-three and from Connecticut, recounted this early experience of being attacked:

> It was the winter of 1985. I was thirteen years old. I was spending my Christmas vacation with my grandparents in Atlanta, Georgia. They lived in an apartment complex that was directly behind a small shopping center. One day I was riding my bike, which my grandparents had given me for Christmas. It was black and gray and almost looked like a scooter. I liked it very much. For some reason, I liked to eat ice cream outside in cold weather, so I decided to ride my bike around the corner to the grocery store to buy some. When I got to the store, I locked my bike up and went in. It took about fifteen minutes to get what I wanted. Once I had paid for my ice cream, I walked out of the store. I saw two or three white boys, who looked around sixteen or seventeen years old, admiring my bike. I walked to my bike and unlocked it. As I began to get on it, I heard one of the boys say, "I sure would like that bike."
>
> Another one said, "I should take the bike from the little nigger." I started to pedal as fast as I could to get away from them. When I got around the corner, I was praying that they weren't behind me. While I was riding in the back parking lot of the store, two boys jumped in front of me from behind a dumpster, and I fell. I was laid out on the ground with my bike on top of me. One of the boys grabbed my bike and started riding it. I remember screaming, "Give me my bike. Give me my bike." He didn't pay any attention. I tried to get up to chase him, but the other white boy knocked me back on the ground saying, "Little black boy, get down on the ground

where you belong." Then he ran away. I could not catch up with the boy on my bike because he was going too fast. When this happened I felt like I had lost my best friend. The result was that I didn't go to Georgia to visit my grandparents as much as I used to. When I did visit them, I rarely left the front of the apartment building.

McKinley, who was twenty-three when we spoke, told me about what happened to him when he was nine years old and living in Sarasota, Florida. His mother and siblings had a craving for sweets one day, and his mother asked him to go to the bakery to purchase some cupcakes and jelly swirls.

The bakery was located about three quarters of a mile from his house. While McKinley was walking back from the bakery with two bags full of goodies, a pick-up truck stopped beside him on the street. McKinley paid no attention to the vehicle until an older white man spat directly in his face and called him "half a nigger" (McKinley has light skin). He threw his two bags at the truck and ran home. With eyes full of tears, he told his mother his sad tale. McKinley told me, "I haven't forgotten that day, and I never will."

As we can see from McKinley's story, spitting is another method that bigoted people use to mark their territory and to show contempt. There are physical expressions of racism that are even more despicable than spitting. Josephat, twenty-two, was walking down the road in Camp Springs, Maryland, when a pick-up truck with three white men in it pulled up beside him. They looked at him for twenty or thirty seconds and then threw a container of human feces at him and called him nigger. Josephat's first reaction was shock, but he became angry and wanted to hurt them back.

He went home, washed off the filth, and called his sister. He was twenty-one when this happened, and his sister was twenty-four. They were not only brother and sister but also best friends. He told her what had happened and about how for the first time in his life he wanted to hurt a white person. She changed the subject and talked about the fun times they had shared. His sister's talk calmed him, and he decided to go through official channels to address the situation instead of going after the men himself. Josephat knew the men who had assaulted him. He got their license number and called the police. The six men were arrested for assault and battery.

Threats and hate crimes evoke anger and other painful feelings. The more personalized the racism, such as in these stories of physical assaults, the more violent and retaliatory the feelings generated in the victim. Yet blacks of all ages usually bear the pain in their hearts—especially the pain caused by a dirty, demeaning, and devastating act like having feces dumped on them. McKinley's story is but one example of this. In Josephat's case, fortunately, his sister helped him take the appropriate actions and not endanger himself further. But the fact that Josephat so strongly desired to get back at the men shows how deep feelings of impotence and rage can run. White adults and children need to find better ways to express themselves and to feel secure about themselves.

WHAT TO DO ABOUT IT

Of course there are many white people who are not bigoted and who behave with integrity. Yet many are silent socially and politically, thereby failing to promote their own convictions and to challenge racist statements and behaviors. But unless such people become both vocal and active, racism will continue to flourish.

Countering racism crosses all political lines. People of integrity can be found in every part of the political spectrum, from the most conservative-minded people to the most progressive. And it is these people—all of them—whom I hope to reach with this book. I learned many years ago that a person's political viewpoint is no indicator of his or her ability to behave with dignity, respect, and fairness toward others. When I was a doctoral student at the University of Virginia, one of my professors, who was white, asked me to have lunch with him in the faculty dining room. While we were walking, he turned to me and said, "I'm a conservative, but I do believe in justice in the academic system." His comment surprised me, because, like most blacks, I had always equated conservatism with racism. His words, which I took to mean that he would give a fair grade to everyone—including me—as long as we worked hard and earned it, suggested otherwise. This honorable professor stayed true to his word, and we've remained friends.

This may seem like a small example. But a main theme of this book is that even what might seem like a trifle to the perpetrator has a profound effect on the victim. Conversely, a kind act or words, like those of my professor, although insubstantial on the surface, can have an equally profound effect. Lives are made up of small acts—either those that tear down and destroy racism—or those that encourage and support justice. That day, on my way to lunch, because of one sentence uttered by my professor, I learned a very valuable lesson: that *anyone*—even the people we least expect—can practice moral and social equality.

What White People Can Do

Countering racism begins at home, that is, in the neighborhoods where we raise our families, where our children grow up. Since the 1960s, American neighborhoods have been rapidly changing. Civil rights legislation gave blacks—for the first time since they arrived on this continent—the chance to move out of projects and ghettos and into the suburbs and other nicer areas. The impact of this type of migration on American neighborhoods has been enormous.

Between 1960 and 1980, as middle-class and upper-middle-class blacks began moving into previously all-white neighborhoods, white families began moving out. Black-to-white ratios in the affected neighborhoods shifted rapidly, with For Sale signs popping up overnight. As soon as the proportion of blacks reached about 60 percent, the remaining white families moved out en masse, leaving behind only those on fixed incomes who could not afford to move.

Not only did these neighborhoods become mostly black, but their new residents overpaid for their new homes. Eager to move somewhere nicer, in many cases the incoming black families paid whatever price the sellers demanded. White realtors became richer, and a few black realtors did as well.

While the past cannot be changed, there is much that can be done now to improve the situation. White realtors can be the first to help by showing all types of neighborhoods to blacks who are house hunting. Many qualified black buyers are shown only houses in black neighborhoods; they should have the right to choose among all the houses available in their price range—not just those that "match their race." Realtors must also show property at one asking price for all buyers. The two-tiered pricing system—one price for blacks, another for whites—although immoral and illegal, is still practiced by many realtors.

The importance of fair housing practices goes far beyond simply being just to blacks. Integrated neighborhoods are an essential tool in creating an open, tolerant society. Only when people of all colors live together will they truly learn about one another. Only by learning about one another can people come to realize that we are all far more alike than we are different. And only then will we be able to truly accept one another as equals.

Whites in integrated neighborhoods can reach out in friendship, welcoming their new black neighbors. It doesn't take much—a casserole, a batch of brownies, some cut flowers—to make someone feel welcome. Such simple gestures can go a long way toward bringing neighbors together and turning strangers into friends. What many white families fail to realize is that many black families are hesitant to make the first gesture of friendship. Racism has taught them to be wary, to expect rejection, and to be cautious about reaching out to whites, which is why it is so important that whites make the first move.

If the newcomers are from out of town, offering tips about good places to shop or local attractions is a great way to help out. White families can look for—and create—social opportunities to get to know their black neighbors better. An invitation for coffee or dessert, a casual card game, a cook-out—all of these are perfect settings for meeting people as people.

Blacks and whites simply need to *talk*. And when people get to know one another in this way—simply as people—they discover how much they really do have in common. Despite the headlines flashing stories about black crime, most people have similar values. Most of us value happiness, good health, and freedom. Most of us value education, financial security, and the opportunity to work creatively and productively.

Of course our cultures differ, but these differences only add to the benefits of getting to know one another. People from every culture have something of value that they can teach to people of other backgrounds. A white colleague once told me, "Blacks need to live around whites to learn what whites have been learning almost four hundred years." He was right, and it works both ways. Black and white Americans alike have information and ideas of enormous value to share. The list is endless, from stock market tips to tips on child-rearing, from recipes to advice on networking in the workplace. We can introduce one another to new types of art and music. We all, individually and culturally, have much of value to offer.

Neighborhood civic leagues are another great way to foster integrated minds and hearts among neighbors. Working side-by-side, listening seriously to one another's ideas, finding solutions to shared problems—what better ways are there for people to discover how similar we all are, that the color of our skin really doesn't matter?

The most important result of getting together also has the potential to be the most lasting. When white neighbors welcome their black neighbors, when black and white families socialize together, the children growing up in these neighborhoods will be forever changed. Absorbing the behavior they see their parents model, they will grow up with open minds, ready to accept each person on his or her own merits rather than judging people on the basis of skin color or other differences. When these children become adults and have children of their own, the lessons of justice, fairness, and kindness will be perpetuated and racism will be on its way out.

Shepherd, who was twenty-seven when we met, had this story to tell:

> I was eight years old in the summer of 1980. I was living in Sarasota, Florida. My family and I had just moved into a new apartment complex. I met Donald, a white boy the same age as me. We became friends the first day we met. Donald and I did almost everything that two wild-eyed eight-year-olds could think of. We spent the whole summer together. Donald became my best friend. Though Donald is white and I'm black, color didn't make any difference.

In many ways, Donald and Shepherd were just ordinary kids. Yet in other ways, they were extraordinary. Suppose everyone in America became just like these children. Color wouldn't matter, and we would be one nation, every individual a welcome part of the whole yet still able to benefit from and to celebrate his or her diversity. It is safe to assume that Donald learned from his parents to be open-minded. Children from well-meaning white families such as Donald's can teach important lessons to us all.

As a child, James, twenty-three and a Connecticut resident, also had a well-intentioned white child as a playmate. What he learned then has stayed with him:

> Because I was the only black child in a white neighborhood, my friends were all white. I have one friend who has been my friend since the first grade. Now I'm a college student. We're more like brothers than friends. We talked about issues instead of letting them fester and cause problems.

James spells out for us what it takes for people to connect as people: communication. He and his friend, Forbes, *talked* to each other, and they still do. We would all do well to follow their example.

As Donald and Shepherd and James and Forbes clearly demonstrate, children can be a powerful force for preventing racism before it begins. My plea is for all white Americans to teach their children to be like Donald and Forbes, to raise their children to respect all people, regardless of color.

It is truly amazing what one well-meaning, self-respecting white person can do for a black family. My husband was looking for a new home in Norfolk, Virginia. When he found a suitable apartment, he asked Ruth, a white work colleague, to inquire about the rent, which she did. Later, he called and inquired himself. Imagine how reassured he felt to be quoted the same price. He rented the apartment. The waterfront apartment was a lovely home for us, but without the help of my husband's white associate, he might never have taken that first step.

There is so much more that individual white people can do. To share an example from my own life, in 1994 I was invited to work at the Patrick Air Force Base in Florida. I was going to be away from my husband and family for an extended period and needed somewhere to live. After helping me find and move into a lovely condominium complex in Indian Harbor Beach, my husband planned to return to his job in Virginia. But while he was helping me settle in, he needed a question answered and rang the bell two doors down. The couple who lived there, who were Jewish, couldn't have been more helpful. And that was just the beginning. After my husband left, I was the only black person in an almost entirely white complex. But Sylvia and Hy soon became my friends—and they remain so to this day.

At first, knowing that I often worked at home, Sylvia would stop by for occasional quick visits. She never telephoned beforehand; we were close enough for her to ring the bell, come in, sit down, and talk. She and I enjoyed many warm chats. Though brief, those visits did much to lift my spirits, break up the monotony, and keep me from feeling lonely. One day, after coming home from a hard day at the base, I answered the door and there stood Sylvia, hot supper in hand. Each encounter between us led to a deeper friendship. I even learned from Sylvia that straining was the secret to clear chicken broth, and I bought two strainers as soon as I returned to Virginia.

That's not all she did for me. Because Sylvia told the condo organization that I played bridge, they began to invite me to their bridge games, where I was accepted warmly and lovingly. Those games opened up new avenues of friendship for me. Sylvia also found me a walking partner, once she discovered that I love brisk walking.

As Sylvia so clearly proved, it takes only one well-meaning white person to help blacks become part of a neighborhood. Once she opened the door, the rest of my neighbors welcomed me in— but it took that one person to get it all started. Sylvia helped me out of friendship, but friendship isn't even necessary. We do not have to like another person to treat him or her fairly. We just have to be people of principles and integrity, willing to actively promote equal treatment to everyone.

Blacks who want to cultivate friendships with whites are not looking for hand-outs. They are not "gimme blacks." On the contrary, they're hard-working black people who simply want to be treated the same way white people are. No one wants to be overcharged for goods and services. Everyone wants to be trusted, included, appreciated. Blacks are not looking for white friends only for what they can gain from them. Rather, they are looking for friendship.

Blacks want to be integrated into their neighborhoods; they don't want to be singled out as "special cases." While many black people value their heritage, they don't always want to be organizing black community groups just to provide opportunities to socialize for themselves and their children. Sometimes they just want to be a part of the community they live in. As I stated earlier, many blacks are just waiting for an overture from their white neighbors.

What Black People Can Do

Blacks, like anyone else, want to share their neighborhoods with friendly people. They want to take care of their homes and keep their property in good shape. They want to watch their children play with other children and make friends as they grow up. Many black people work actively to develop good relationships with white friends, acquaintances, and neighbors. Friendship between blacks and whites is invaluable. It enables people of both races to feel good about themselves and to outgrow their personal insecurities.

Of course some blacks do not choose to pursue relationships with white people. Fearing rejection, they keep to themselves. Knowing from bitter experience that many white people treat blacks poorly, they are unable to trust even the whites who mean well. Not knowing whether these whites are genuine, they close themselves off rather than risk being hurt or mistreated again.

But having good relations with even a few white people can be of great—and practical—value to a black person. At work, in the neighborhood, on community boards and associations, in the school system, a well-meaning white person can break the ice for a black person, can speak up on their behalf, and can offer assistance and practical support. And as I stated earlier, it is a person's integrity, not his or her political persuasion, that matters.

This is a shared journey, of course. Just as white Americans must learn to reach out in friendship to their black neighbors, blacks must learn how to respond positively. As we learn, we will all get better at this important business of building a fair and open society. With practice, more and more black people can become comfortable with making the first move. Blacks can continue learning to accept a white person's genuine offer of friendship. In a shared journey, black and white friendships can take beautiful directions. Sylvia and I are just one example.

Our friendship was reciprocal, just like other black-white friendships. Sylvia was wealthy and had many friends in the condominium complex. She shared those friends with me. I, in turn, enhanced her status because Colonel Joe at the Patrick Air Force Base in Florida sent me to Fort Leavenworth to do research at the federal prison. She felt good about my living in an officer's suite in the building where General Colin Powell had stayed to dedicate the Buffalo Soldier monument in 1992 at Fort Leavenworth. The bronze statue of a mounted Buffalo Soldier honors the black soldiers who comprised the 9th and 10th Cavalry Regiments. They were among the first all-black regiments in the United States. General Powell honored the bravery of soldiers who were given their name by Indians. In 1994, I learned about the justice that black, white, and Hispanic men received in the military justice system.

When I returned to Patrick Air Force Base and gave a lecture on that research, Sylvia and some of our neighbors attended. Neighbors who learned about the lecture too late complained that they hadn't been invited. Patrick Air Force Base officials thanked my neighbors for attending the lecture and acknowledged their appreciation for that link between the base and the community. One friendship, between a black and a white, touched the military institution and the lives of many civilian employees and community residents very positively. Blacks, with the initiative of whites, can help solve the problem of racism through healthy friendships. The key is for whites to take the initiative. A majority of blacks will share fulfilling life experiences with white people.

2

FROM DAY CARE
TO GRADUATE SCHOOL

Black people have always had a deep desire for education. Even the slaves, most of whom missed out on schooling, took advantage of every opportunity to get an education. "Many a sympathetic person taught slaves to read. In some cases, private teachers were bold enough to maintain Negro schools." These schools were organized in Savannah, Georgia; Charleston, South Carolina; and Norfolk, Virginia.[1] Other slaves learned from other educated slaves and from influential white men and children whom they accompanied to school; servants learned from ministers and officials for whom they worked.[2]

During the Civil War, some slaves escaped to or were brought within Union lines and were educated by northern blacks. Mrs. Mary Chase, a free Negro of Alexandria, Virginia, opened the first school for contrabands on September 1, 1861, and two weeks later, Mrs. Mary Peake, another black woman, opened the first freedmen's aid societies' school sponsored by the American Missionary Association near Fortress Monroe, Virginia.[3]

These individual efforts and formal schools enabled some slaves and runaways to the North to learn how to read and write—an activity threatening to the cause of keeping blacks down. "In 1854 there was found in Norfolk, Virginia, what the radically proslavery people considered a dangerous white woman. It was discovered that one Mrs. Douglas and her daughter had for three years been teaching a school maintained for education of Negroes." Mrs. Douglas and her pupils were charged and then acquitted with the understanding that she would not commit this offense again. Her crime had been to educate blacks, which was illegal during slavery.[4]

Blacks were emancipated in 1863, almost one hundred fifty years ago. The second stage in their struggle to obtain an education began immediately afterward. A major challenge to blacks in the South was the economic system of sharecropping, a system that remained in place into the 1950s. To succeed, it required illiterate, hardworking, and compliant blacks. Sharecropping was a southern farming system whereby black workers rented a portion of land to farm. There were regional variations. Often the landowner furnished the land and a team of animals to pull the plows and cultivators. The farmers paid for fertilizer and pesticides; they also did all the work. On some plantations, the white landowners owned stores. The sharecroppers bought all their wares at these stores, charging their purchases. At the end of each season, the landowner deducted the price of goods purchased and any money the sharecroppers had borrowed from their earnings. The remainder—usually between $75 and $300—constituted the sharecropper's income for the year.

How did a large family live on such a meager income? Most families used two strategies. First, they produced their own food. In the summer, between hoeing and harvesting, the women and children canned fruits and vegetables. They also dried fruit. The men raised hogs and the women raised chickens, providing meat and eggs. If they owned a cow, then they had a large amount of clabber (curdled milk) that could be churned into butter. Second, when they were finished hoeing their rented land or picking their cotton or processing their tobacco, they were hired by the landowner to farm a portion of the land that the landowner had reserved for himself. On a successful plantation, sharecroppers earned $3 a day or $3 for every hundred pounds of cotton they picked.

Essentially, this system prevented school-aged black males and females from attending full school years. While the boys stayed home to help plow and harvest, the girls were kept out of school so that they could help pick cotton, shake the dirt off plowed-up peanuts for stacking, and process tobacco leaves. Because harvesting occurred in late summer and in the fall, black children missed one to two months of classes at the beginning of every school year. And because the crops were ready to be hoed in late spring, many black children were also kept out of school the last few weeks of the school year.

Although most blacks today have left behind their share-cropper pasts, many black children are still deprived of a good education. The establishment of neighborhood schools, for example, separates black and white children because few blacks live in white neighborhoods. Because the budgets for many of these schools directly mirror the neighborhoods' income, few black schools are as well equipped as white schools.

After schools were integrated by federal mandate, black test scores soared. When they were resegregated, the scores dropped. Neither form of schooling affected white students' scores on standardized tests. A few metropolitan cities created magnet and gifted schools for whites and a handful of blacks. These schools are not a substitute for integrated education for all children. Black children all over America need to attend school with whites to gain the motivation and competitive spirit that they missed while their ancestors were working in the fields and performing other low-paying jobs. When black students are given equal learning experiences (eye contact, solid teaching, warmth, fair grades, friendships, a well-equipped school, and prepared teachers), they grow as motivated and competitive as white students.

It is crucial for black students to compete in schools with white students. White schools are better equipped, teachers, white and black, are better instructors, and the competition is keener. That is the basis for a good education.

The usual picture of black neighborhood schools is poorly prepared teachers, lethargic teachers and pupils, nonexistent or broken-down equipment, absence of foreign-language labs, lack of computers or too few computers, poorly appointed teachers' lounges (all teachers deserve comfortable rest areas), and buildings or trailers in need of repair. That is the foundation for a poor education. The exceptions to these realities are too few to warrant discussion here.

Perhaps one of the most insidious forms of discrimination against blacks in schools is the tracking system, in which white students are placed in college-track courses and black students are placed in vocational training or other nonacademic courses. As a result, black students are often denied college entrance because they lack advanced English, science, and mathematics. Some black students attempt to overcome the effects of this system. They attend colleges that enroll students with numerous deficiencies and spend six to eight years earning a college degree. So many black college students start their careers one to four years behind white students their own age—a real injustice.

An equally insidious form of discrimination against blacks in school is the special education program. For decades, capable black students and black troublemakers in regular classes have been placed in special education classes. Denise Watson Batts, a news reporter, said in the *Virginian-Pilot*, "Walk into some special-education classes in South Hampton Roads (Norfolk, Chesapeake, Portsmouth, Virginia Beach, and Suffolk, Virginia cities) and it quickly becomes apparent: Most of the children are black. In each of the given school divisions, black children are more likely than whites to be labeled mildly retarded and placed into special classes for slow learners." Batts found in Chesapeake that "black children make up 35 percent of the student body, but more than 70 percent of the students identified as 'educable mentally retarded.'" She stated that officials can't explain the difference between the races, but said poverty, not race, "is a serious factor in special-education referrals." Batts cited another view: "Some parents and education experts believe that special education is another form of segregation."[5]

Because we know that special education classes were small in large high schools before desegregation, and because many teachers agree with the reasons I stated earlier for the sharp rise in special-education enrollment, there is no doubt that special-education classes are another racist way that white school officials discourage and impede the education of black children.

In the mid-1990s, I conducted a study of black males who had dropped out of the five high schools in Norfolk, Virginia. In at least one of the high schools, the administrators, teachers, and counselors did not make it known throughout the black student population that advanced classes were available to good students. The white students were informed their freshman year, which encouraged them to work hard to get enrolled in the prestigious courses. This behavior is part and parcel of the tracking system and special-education programs, and it severely handicaps black students.

Clifton, a twenty-three-year-old student in Norfolk, was one of the few exceptions at his high school. Although he made it into these special classes, the lack of support for black students got in his way:

> I left school in the tenth grade because of my designated gifted and talented courses. My white counselor suggested that I take the courses and warned that they would be difficult. I took history, science, and algebra for the gifted and put too much on myself. I thought that I could manage and hang in there. In these classes, they don't check homework. As a result, I slacked up because I knew they weren't checking papers. Finally, I dropped science and kept history and algebra.
>
> When I was enrolled in all three gifted classes, I did a little science, read history, and studied algebra. If the teachers

had said read hard, I would have done so. Since they didn't, I mostly looked and glanced over the work. I didn't know we would have so many pages on the test. I could've managed, but I'm not the kind of person who stays in the house studying hours and hours every page in all my books and learning every detail—without definite assignments. I skimmed and read a couple of pages. In history, I read almost everything. I didn't read science much, but I kept trying to catch up with the other students.

My grades fell. I received an E (a failing grade) in science, a D in history, and a C in algebra. I was set back, because I was expecting to graduate without an E. I dropped out of school because of these grades. I kept thinking about them.

If there had been more blacks in the classes, that would have made me do better. There were only two other blacks in the classes. It made me feel uncomfortable. They, too, must have felt strange. If there had been an equal number of blacks and whites in my classes, I would've made it. Even the teachers were white.

Also, when I talked about my gifted and talented classes, I learned that most of the blacks at school had never heard of them. The people at my school probably didn't tell blacks about the courses because they didn't want black students to be successful.

I got along with the whites in my classes, but we weren't friends who could visit and see each other after school. This experience caused me to switch roles. I related to the white students in my classes on their terms and to my black friends on their terms. That is, when I was with my black friends, I tried to be hip. But I couldn't make a good friend in the gifted and talented classes. I felt they didn't want me in there because I knew about racism. They were so unfriendly to me, I know they were prejudiced. Some of them wouldn't even associate with me. When we discussed slavery in my history class, sometimes white students laughed. I didn't see anything funny. They probably thought they were better than the three of us. Because they were in the majority, they had the upper hand. I felt they didn't want me to make it. I didn't think anybody cared about me. I couldn't go over to their houses and study. I was thinking about asking the teachers to tutor me, but I didn't.[6]

Clifton raises many important points. To begin with, the black students weren't friends and didn't bond and help each other learn their lessons. Black students need to practice mutual self-help. They should realize that there is academic strength in collective studying. It is vital that they learn to enjoy seeing each other succeed—friend, acquaintance, or stranger.

Clifton speaks volumes about the differences between whites and blacks in the formal and informal opportunities to get an education. Schools must be sure to educate all students about the full range of class requirements and opportunities. In Clifton's case, few blacks at his high school had heard about classes for the gifted and talented. Had they known, perhaps more would have worked harder to earn the honor. Further, because there were many more whites than blacks in his classes, Clifton did not feel comfortable enough to explore, experiment, or test his abilities, or even to ask for the help that he needed.

Although Clifton clearly knew what was needed to succeed in the courses, he suggests that he was not disciplined enough by his instructors. Black students need clear assignments and instructions and to have their papers corrected and returned. It is important for teachers to correct their homework and tests and to make constructive suggestions and comments. Otherwise, black students cannot reach their full potential in their courses.

Clifton felt the white students in his classes were prejudiced and that he was not wanted. This sense of being unwanted also influenced his performance. He didn't feel a part of his classes.

After school, his classmates didn't study with him. Neither black nor white students excel in an unfriendly classroom. Most black students do not excel academically without friendship. They, like white students, need friendship that extends beyond classrooms.

Certainly it is critical that black students be made aware of the full range of academic possibilities at their schools and should be encouraged to stay in high school and in the advanced programs. Clifton clearly makes a case for the importance of keeping the classroom as integrated as possible, and the best way to achieve this is by giving black students the opportunity to participate in all types of classes and by encouraging them to work hard and to finish school.

DAY CARE AND PRESCHOOL

Clifton, whose struggle was in the early 1990s, is not alone. Today, black students still struggle with racism in the classroom, which starts with day care and follows them through graduate school. Tricia, a college student who was twenty-five and a Maryland resident when I interviewed her, described this experience:

> It was 1992, and I was living in Lyons, Georgia. I was telephoning day-care centers to locate openings. On the telephone, I was given all the information I needed. As soon as my daughter and I entered the first center, I knew something was wrong. Everyone stared at us. When I asked to speak to the people in charge, I was told they were not in and that there were no openings. This same incident occurred at six different day-care centers. I was unable to keep my job, because I couldn't get child care for my daughter. My reaction was shock. I didn't know that white racism was directed toward black babies. I became frustrated and angry. I've never overcome that experience. After that, I moved back to my hometown, Baltimore.

Tricia had a "white voice." Once the day-care personnel saw her, they realized they had mistaken her for a white woman. Most important, adult whites refused to permit an innocent black baby from sharing day care with innocent white babies. Tragically, the workers laid the foundation for the babies to become racists.

Recall from the last chapter Sonya's experience with the two white boys taunting a black boy who wanted to play. One of the boys later confessed that he had learned the word *nigger* at day care. Sadly, black children encounter racism at a tender age when they are denied the opportunity to attend day-care centers that are owned and operated by whites. And this racism is spread by equally young children—children at day-care centers—who don't know any better.

Racism doesn't die in the lives of children after they leave day care. Rather, it continues to make a deeper and deeper impression on the children at every stage of their lives, including at preschool. Debbie, a twenty-seven-year-old ROTC student at Norfolk State University and a resident of Virginia, told me about her daughter's experience at preschool:

> The third most racist experience that I've had occurred recently. I experienced it through my three-year-old daughter. One day at preschool, the students had a "show and tell." All the students had brought their toys to school. My daughter forgot her toys, so I had to go home and get them. My daughter told me specifically what to bring. She wanted her pretty black Barbie doll with the white dress. She loved this doll and thought that it was pretty and often said, "When I grow up, I want to look just like my Barbie."
>
> All the other children were white. While my daughter brought out her Barbie during show and tell, they screwed up their faces and said, "Yuck. That's not Barbie. She's ugly."
>
> Afterward, Jennie's love for her Barbie changed. Did love for herself change? One day I'll find out. I think that I was more devastated than Jennie. Even though she cried for

hours and never carried her doll to school again, I couldn't believe those little children's actions. That was racism by babies, so to speak.

As a result, I made sure that my daughter knew that she was beautiful and that her dolls and family were beautiful. Every day, before she went to school, I spoke of her beauty and loveliness. I did my best to be sure that she would not develop low self-esteem. Even so, I feel that that experience will stick with her the rest of her life.

Jennie was three years old when she was hurt by other children her age. Where did little three-year-old children learn not to like the color black? They learned it from their parents and from their older sisters and brothers in their own homes. The origin of racism is in the family. Racist teachings take on a life that is carried on by the children from generation to generation. If white families educated their children about race earlier on, by giving them dolls of all different colors to teach them equality, for example, then this chain of racism could be broken.

ELEMENTARY SCHOOL

Racism also rears its ugly head among the children at elementary school, as the following stories indicate. The students in my study reported time and again something they remembered learning at that stage: that white teachers did not like black children being the best students in the class. Lawton, who was twenty-one years old when we spoke and a resident of Florida, told me what occurred when he was in third grade:

> I was nine years old and attended a predominantly white school. In one class, I was one of two black students. I sat in the front of the class, so that I could learn. When my white female teacher taught the lessons and asked the class whether

we had questions, I raised my hand. She looked over me as if she saw neither me nor my hand. However, the first time we took a test, I earned an A.

One afternoon, she asked me to stay after class to talk about my grades. First, she asked me if I had cheated on the test. I said no. She gave me an oral test. I answered every question correctly, including the questions that I had missed on the first test. The next day, she assigned me another seat in the back of the classroom. At the time I didn't pay it any attention. Soon I started complaining that I wasn't learning anything in the back of the class, and she responded by saying, "Just do your best."

I told my mother, and she went to the school the next day and asked why I had been moved from the front of the class to the back. The teacher replied, "He was cheating." I couldn't believe that she lied. At that moment, I realized that for some reason she didn't want me to learn. I couldn't think of any other way to get back to the front of the class, because I was black and there were only two of us in the class. The situation kind of ruined me mentally at the young age of nine because, at that time, I felt like I had done something wrong.

Lawton, like Clifton, found himself a minority in class. Unlike Clifton, he was at first able to navigate the situation. He sat in the front of the class and aced the first test. That was his first crime, which brought a sentence with consequences that will most likely last a lifetime. When the teacher retested him alone, in a situation in which he had no chance to cheat or even to read the questions, and found him to be even smarter the second time than the first; that was his second crime.

As a penalty, Lawton's teacher found a way to keep him from getting good grades. Children in the back of the classroom are often less attentive than students in the front, and no doubt, they distracted Lawton. It is also harder to hear from the back, and

Lawton realized that he was not learning. Even though he was only in the third grade, Lawton realized that his white teacher did not want him to learn. Black children face racism so early that they learn to recognize it as early as third grade. How? Their parents warn them to be on the lookout for different treatment, an experience that in itself is painful for black children. Just as white children learn racism at home, black children learn to recognize it at home as well.

Other students described the racism they encountered at elementary school, both from other students and from their teachers. Josh, who was nineteen when I interviewed him, related what happened at his predominantly white school in Great Falls, Montana, when he was ten years old and in the fourth grade:

> While I attended the school in Montana, my teacher placed the students in her class in certain groups. Those groups were designed to enhance our reading skills. Each group level was assigned a color based on how well they read. The white students were put in the higher-level group (yellow), while the black and Hispanic students were placed in the lower-level group (orange). I asked the teacher if I could be placed in the yellow group. My teacher claimed that the orange group was appropriate for my reading ability. I didn't press the issue because I thought that I couldn't change my status. However, I strove to read better at the lower level.

White people are often creative in their racism. Josh's teacher didn't try to keep her bigotry a secret and used colors to separate the minority students from the white students. Elementary children know their colors. When they are used against them, they know that too. The injustice was so vivid that Josh even questioned being placed in the lower-level group. Josh, only a fourth grader, was forced to fight his teacher's ugly behavior. Even though he was not able to change his status, Josh wanted to read better at the lower level than the students read on the higher level. That is precisely the attitude that some black children must take if they are to succeed both in school and in society. But that is not the only answer to success. Black school children can't fight white adult racism alone. Their parents must be prepared to help them. When black parents are unprepared to go to school and confront the racism perpetrated against their children, they should find friends and acquaintances to help resolve the issues. It's their duty to ensure that their children enjoy a supportive school environment, get good grades, and learn worthwhile information.

MIDDLE SCHOOL

The young men and women I interviewed had stories to tell about how prejudice and discrimination continued to dog them as they left grade school and continued on to junior high. Joe, now a twenty-year-old college student, was a fourteen-year-old eighth grader in a Chesapeake, Virginia, junior high school, where a small, isolated incident between a black student and a white student had taken place. One thing led to another, and a fight broke out. While the fight was being broken up, racial slurs were exchanged. Tensions were already high, and the trashy talk echoed through the student body. A race riot then broke out. Julian, twenty-one, shed this light on the riot:

> One must realize that the school was basically a white school, which was integrated approximately ten years earlier. One should also realize that the area around the school was still all white and that there were some whites who still believed that "if it ain't white, it ain't right." My reaction to this situation was anger. It was awful to arrive at school in the morning and run into whiter-than-we individuals calling me a nigger and my black female friends "black bitches." Remember, we were all fourteen- and fifteen-year-old kids. It tended to force us into

a free-for-all fight. Trust me. Anger came to the surface very, very quickly, and before it was over, the white individual who called me nigger was almost beaten into the ground. Most people react according to the way they feel, and I felt angry.

I later felt shocked about the whole scenario, because really, I didn't know at the time what was going on. I knew I was approached in a bad way; therefore, I reacted on the basis of my first instinct. The result of the situation was that many students were suspended from school for days, even weeks.

In this Virginia school, a black student and a white student started a race riot—an entire school engaging in violence. Racial slurs cause a good deal of racial tension in the hearts and minds of blacks; occasionally the struggle escalates into violence. More often the struggle causes them to avoid whites as much as possible. That's the only way they know to keep their feelings from getting hurt. The result is that they never reach their fullest academic potential. They even fail socially, isolating themselves in lunchroom and library settings—understandably so. They do not want to be around mean-spirited whites. Rather than flourish, black students feel dwarfed by white students' negative reactions to them.

HIGH SCHOOL

Racism toward students does not stop in middle school. Sadly, many white high school teachers often have a negative view of their black students. White school teachers are some of the strongest perpetrators of racism. They are motivated to display racism toward blacks for many reasons. They fear and dislike their skin color. White people, teachers included, need to acknowledge that they have no reason to fear black people's skin color. And they use that fear as an excuse to practice racism.

White teachers also display racist behaviors to teach them to their students. They make certain that racism is perpetuated from one generation to the next. Further, a majority of white teachers do not want to see black students excel. They prove it on every academic level by awarding students at least one letter grade lower than they earned, by acting unkind and ignoring them—they don't hang their posters in coveted locations in the classroom, for example—and by not giving black achievers the same recognition they give white achievers. White teachers understand exactly what they are doing. They recognize that their racism effectively discourages some black students from reaching their highest academic peaks. That should not be what they want to do. They should want to help all students, black or white, find their true potential.

Juniper, nineteen and from Virginia, told this story about his teacher:

> During my senior year in high school, I was assigned an English class taught by a white woman. My father had been a teacher at my high school and had died the previous year. Of course, I was prone to be upset. My reputation was not as good as it should have been; I was known as the class clown and didn't have the best grades.
>
> One day it was my turn to give a report to my English class. When I finished, the teacher shot me an incriminating look and said in a disdainful voice, "This must be some type of sick joke." I was shocked. What could I have done to her to elicit such a remark? In fact, I asked myself this question during the rest of the class. Later in other classes and even as I drove home, I asked myself that question. Those same eight words rang through my head.
>
> When I got home, I waited for my mom and told her the situation. The next day she went to the high school to see the teacher and the principal. That class was never easy, but after my mom talked with her, the teacher never made any more of those comments.

Sometimes no matter how hard black students work, they are forced to contend with unequal treatment in the classroom. Many students I spoke with reported that their white teachers often overlooked them in class, calling only on the white students to recite or to answer questions. Or teachers who wanted to annoy a black student would call on him or her repeatedly. The students also reported the unwillingness of their white teachers to give them extra help. Often when they approached their teachers for help, they were put off and told to come back. More often than not, black students, especially males, who generally do not want to risk a blow to their egos, never returned to their teachers to ask for needed help.

Although most of the students I spoke with endured this kind of racism for an entire course, often without complaining, every now and then, one protested. Clemson, a twenty-one-year-old student from New Jersey, described how he fought back:

> I was in my freshman year of high school in New York City. In my mathematics class, there were a lot of students, but there were more whites than blacks. It was difficult because the teacher was also white. My teacher, Mrs. Jenson, used to act like she was above everybody else. She had favorites in the class. I would raise my hand, and she would look over me to call on someone else. I would go to her for help, and she would tell me to come back. When the white kids went to her for help, she would give it.
>
> The same stuff kept happening to me. I told my parents about it, and they talked with the teacher. However, she kept doing the same things. I was upset with her. Finally, I asked her, in front of the whole class, "Do you like black people?" After I did that, everything started getting better.

At first Clemson was embarrassed and hurt because the teacher failed to call on him. Then his struggle became so difficult that he had to speak out. For students to learn, they need to feel in control of their environment. Clearly, Clemson was not in control of his; his teacher was. When black students are forced to defend themselves against racism in class, as Clemson was, it interferes with a normal classroom experience. Fortunately, Clemson was able to regain some control in his class, but he should not have had to contend with such a situation in the first place.

Being treated as though they are invisible hurts the feelings of black students and contributes to their sense of inferiority. In effect, these white teachers who mistreat their black students indicate their own sense of inferiority; they count their black students as invisible so that they can feel superior to them. For regardless of race or ethnic group, people who have high self-esteem are able to treat others with respect and dignity.

When I conducted my study of high school dropouts,[7] I was shocked to discover how many white high school teachers used racist language with their black students. To illustrate, one student I talked with was supposed to be in a certain class, but he was talking with a friend in a different class. The white teacher told him, "Get out of here before I kick your butt." An exchange of words ensued, and the student received a fifteen-day suspension. He never returned to school. Essentially, a teacher's language sabotaged a young black boy's school career. Some would reason that the student could have reacted differently to his teacher. But how different might the result have been if the teacher had simply said something like, "It's time to leave now."

Lester, twenty-one, described another vivid experience of discrimination in his high school:

> I was a rising junior who had developed a great appreciation for music. I had begun writing and directing music for my high school and jazz bands. Many of my friends' parents and directors from other local high schools congratulated me. I decided to audition for drum major.

Conflict developed because the white female director at my school had a philosophy that would not allow me to head the all-white band. My high school, in Churchland, Virginia, had never had a black drum major. It resulted from the paranoid notion that a black drum major would cause the band to "fade to black." I found out that the director accepted this traditional concept.

When I auditioned, I received the highest score, but only received a "second fiddle" position. I did behind-the-scenes work: teaching and writing music with no recognition. The first time that I was denied the position of drum major, I felt betrayed. I had trusted my director as a friend and many of the band parents. For me, love had no color.

When I didn't make the audition, at first I felt that there was something that I hadn't done. When I learned that it was because of my skin color, I realized that my dreams would be a mystery to whites, meaning that whites would not understand my success. They only think of white success. That's not right. I decided to achieve on my own for my people. My people, to me, means all people who despise and are against all forms of racism. My band director tried to explain her reason by saying that the Band Parents Association (mostly white) was not "ready" for a black drum major. She said that the school had a traditional style, and if I were to become drum major, the school would lose respect.

The following year I decided to try out again. This time, I was told that I had to get permission from the principal, assistant principal, and a few band parents. No one had ever done that before. I assumed someone was trying to get someone else to deny me the opportunity to break a racial tradition. Well, I obtained the various permissions, but not without strife. Since it had not been done before, the principal and others were concerned about the process. Furthermore, they were surprised that I didn't get the position the first time I tried out for it.

They knew I deserved it. They have a stereotypical opinion that blacks are musically inclined. That had long been an area accepted by whites. The higher-ups were surprised that a teacher wouldn't let a black excel in music.

Basically, the judges scored us from one to ten in the various categories they made up, like writing music, directing music, teaching music, and marching techniques. Mind you, I had done all those things before I ever auditioned.

During my interview, I explained to the judges what had happened the year before and hinted that I knew that I had won this time and would drop band if I didn't win without a legitimate reason. I won.

At first, I was paranoid, but when my band showed they had confidence in me, that was all I needed. I was there for them, writing and teaching music. They marched until they sweated blood for me, and together we won band competitions. Under my leadership, the band won competitions that it had never won before. The band was appreciated by blacks and by even more whites. More blacks joined the band, and more white students had fun with music. Black students and white students should be given an equal chance to excel. That would benefit teachers, schools, and communities.

When I became drum major, my director advised me to drop algebra and chemistry and take music classes to free up more time to help her. She went to the office, changed my classes, and said it was for my benefit. I needed those classes for college. Consequently, I changed them back with a smile and told her, "No hard feelings, but I would rather learn something."

Lester's story speaks volumes about what goes on in many high schools, even today. First he indicates that in predominantly white schools certain positions, such as drum major, are reserved for whites. Next he demonstrates that blacks can do better than whites but fail to reap the rewards. Instead, they are put behind the scenes,

and less qualified white students are put out front. The band director feared that a black drum major would change the complexion
of the band. She was afraid of what the band parents association
would say, denoting that she felt the same way they did. She did not
struggle for the good of blacks, and her denial of what Lester had
earned caused him to feel betrayed. The pain that he felt over this
betrayal was made all the worse by the fact that Lester had trusted
and loved his band director before this incident. Fortunately, Lester
possessed refreshing common sense. He wanted to perform for his
people—all people who are against racism.

Sadly, it is a common racist practice to require blacks to do
more than whites to get ahead. The next year, even the principal
at Lester's school was surprised that he had to get permission from
so many people to try out again for drum major. And even after
Lester became drum major, his struggle continued. It was only after
he had made the band the best that it had ever been that the struggle ended. This is the fate of many black high school students
who face daily racism. To succeed, they must be better than all the
white students who have gone before them. Even in the end, Lester
had to be strong enough to change his schedule back to college
preparatory classes after the band director had altered his schedule
to meet her needs. She was obviously very threatened by a black
person's success.

In a similar vein, some students I spoke with told me about
being discouraged from pursuing a particular profession, even when
they were qualified and highly motivated. Many were told by their
white school counselors that those occupations were not suitable
for blacks. Amos, a twenty-three-year-old student from Pennsylvania, described one of these experiences.

> My white counselor told me that I either had to be an athlete
> or an entertainer and that I couldn't become a psychiatrist.
> She tried to limit my ability. She said those things to me
> because she was speaking out of ignorance and allowing the

devil to use her. After she tried to stereotype me, I told her
that I can become whatever I want to and left.

Racism in the counselor's office is nothing new. A case in point
is Bill Gaines, who at age fifteen dropped out of school because his
white counselor had told him that his ambition to become a bus
driver, railway engineer, or a hockey or golf player was not possible.
It was the 1950s, and the counselor explained to Gaines that neither of those jobs was for blacks and that the games he played were
not games that blacks play. Gaines didn't let such poor advice prevent him from working his way from a $48-a-week janitorial job to
a $13,500-a-year management job at a housing project in Boston.
His job pride and satisfaction are evident in his remark: "I would
have called anyone a crazy nut who said I'd ever make $13,500 a
year" (an engineer's salary at the time). Yet it is possible that if his
counselor had encouraged and helped him to pursue his goals, he
could have made much more—and completed his degree.[8] Gaines
had his experience in the 1950s, Amos in the 1990s. Amos was
emboldened by his counselor's poor advice. He was determined to
attend college and to become his best.

Traditionally athletic coaches are among the most revered
people at high schools. Many of them go out of their way to
befriend the black students on their teams and to help them succeed in school. Yet many of the young people I interviewed
described their negative experiences with their coaches, who did
not behave much better than the teachers and counselors we have
heard about above. Laskin, a twenty-three-year-old student from
Illinois, told me his story:

> I tried out for the basketball team, and it was clear that I was
> one of the top three players in the gym. Aside from one guy,
> I beat everybody in the games and in shooting. When I played
> in team competition, I also did great. My team won the
> tournament. I was the leading scorer. During my senior year

in high school, I was highly recruited. Everyone knew that I had talent. But the white coach acted as though he didn't want me on his team because I was black. I got cut, along with other good black players, from the team. The whole team was white, and there were boys on the team who had never even played basketball. As a result of this experience, I transferred to another school and played against those guys.

This is another familiar theme in racism: When white people want to keep their group exclusively white, they exclude blacks, even at the expense of success. In those groups, they talk about blacks and attempt to feel good by being in an all-white group. That is racism. Whites need to realize that *no* racism—white *or* black—can give anyone a genuinely good feeling about themselves.

Many black high school students also experience white resistance to their excelling academically and feel they have to work twice as hard to get anywhere. Carlton, a twenty-year-old student, told this story. In his sophomore year of high school, he had transferred from a predominantly black public school to a white Catholic private school. He performed much better at his new school. Carlton told me about the difficulty he experienced as a result of his academic excellence.

In the South, we have boys' and girls' delegation teams. That is, each school sends a team of exceptionally well-rounded, high achievers to New Orleans. They compete in drafting political platforms, discussing social issues, giving political speeches, or whatever. I was chosen for our delegation team on the basis of my academics, not my skin color. Apparently, my white team members didn't think so. I was treated like an outcast the entire trip. At the time, I was living in Shreveport, Louisiana, which is about five hours from New Orleans. I was called a "token" by my teammates. They said that the only way our team could be eligible to participate in the contest was to have at least one black student. My teammates' decision only made me more determined to excel in my part of the competition—debating. When we got to the hotel, I locked myself in the bathroom for four hours and practiced my speech, clearing my voice of unneeded diction problems, concentrating on the words and my thoughts. Needless to say, I won first place in my category, as did a couple of my teammates. What's funny is that I received more appreciation from the white guys whom I beat than from my teammates. I suppose my teammates had improper home training, which made them look at me in a different manner. Fortunately, my parents taught me at an early age how to combat racism. Therefore, I was determined not to let their harassment deter me from my mission.

Carlton carried a double burden. He not only had to prove that he was as gifted and talented as any white student at his school, but he also had to concentrate on all the various events at the conference.

Sometimes this type of racism, treating black people like tokens, invades personal relationships between black and white students at high schools. Watson, a twenty-year-old from Montana, explained:

I went to a predominantly white high school. I thought that white people were my friends, and I trusted them. That was a big mistake. For example, I was close friends with a white boy. He would tell me things, and I would tell him things too.

One day he turned on me. He started telling lies about me. People were becoming angry at me and said that this student had told them things that I had allegedly said. I didn't believe them until the guy picked a fight with me. He said that he should not have associated with a black person anyway. I didn't understand because I had not done anything to him. Later, I found out that he had wanted to be my friend just so that he could get on the football team. He didn't like black people; he just wanted to use me.

Unfortunately, many blacks have had this type of experience. What makes these experiences especially difficult is that the black students have not done anything to cause the rift in the friendship; rather, they discover that whites befriend them only to get something. These black students are not valued as people; they are used for their skin color.

COLLEGE AND GRADUATE SCHOOL

Though we might think that at college, especially at the graduate level, abuse of black students would taper off, frequently it does not. Some of the students I interviewed also experienced racism in their peer relationships at college. Dennis, who was twenty-one when we spoke, attended an integrated college. When he had difficulty with assignments in his math class, he turned to a fellow student, who was white, and asked for help. The student said to him, "I'm not going to help a nigger."

Yet just like in grade, middle, and high school, not all racist behavior at college comes from white peers; some of it comes from adults to whom black parents entrust their children. Claude, twenty, described this experience with his choir master:

> I attended Covington College in New York City and became a member of the singing chorus. At first, I felt out of place because there were only five blacks in the chorus. But after I got to know everyone, I felt more comfortable. During several weeks of warm-ups and notes, we began to see who could sing solo. The white male chorus director told everyone that the person with the best voice would win the job as soloist. We held the auditions in a room full of nonmusical students to get a natural reaction from the crowd. Jack was the first to audition. He sounded good, but not great. I was the last person to be called. As a result, I knew that I had to rock because everyone had heard many different voices.

After my song was over, I was shocked at the loud and long applause. I had really lit up the place. Later that evening, the chorus director crowned Jack the official soloist. When I asked him how he could do that, he only said that I had talent, but my voice didn't suit the songs. I had to wait a whole year, while singing backup before I had another chance to show what I could do. It was at the school's star-search contest that I beat Jack and showed everyone who was really supposed to be the official soloist.

A major problem for black college students is the low percentage of blacks on many college campuses. At first Claude felt uneasy about being one of only five blacks in his college chorus, and this uneasiness hindered his performance. But as he grew more comfortable, he decided to become the chorus soloist. Ironically, traditional racists attitudes should have supported such an undertaking, since so many whites believe that all blacks can sing. But of course not all racial stereotypes work in a candidate's favor.

In fact, Claude's chorus master gave a new twist to the old stereotype. He was saying, in effect, that Claude couldn't sing white folks' music. Yet the next year Claude competed again with the soloist and won. Can you imagine the struggle he went through, for a whole year, with not being selected as the soloist the first time? Can you imagine the preparation it took to sing "white" music better than a white student? Claude had to prove twice that he was the best soloist in his chorus. That is the nature of racism: It makes blacks work twice as hard as whites for the same accolades.

And at college, the struggles aren't just with activities like music or sports. The students I talked to also encountered racism in the classroom, just like they had in high school and earlier. Although the white professors have often earned the highest possible degree in their fields, that does not stop them from mistreating their black students. Frequently, the students reported not receiving the grades they deserved; their comments in class were not recognized, and their professors made little or no eye contact with them. In addition, the professors responded more kindly to questions from white students than from blacks. Even when their professors are black, black students can't always find relief. So many black professors are more helpful and kinder to white students than they are to black students. White teachers in historically black colleges are not exempt from practicing racism. Black university administrators shouldn't retain white faculty members who practice racism against black students in their classrooms. It is the duty of university administrators to protect black students by getting out of their offices and finding out what's going on at the grass-roots level of their universities. They need to recognize that there is what I call an American black student dilemma in this country and in their colleges. Morrison, nineteen and from Illinois, described a common type of insensitivity found among college professors:

My second worst racist experience occurred while I was attending Kensington University in Illinois. I was an eighteen-year-old freshman. Kensington was a predominantly white college; only 10 percent of the student body was black. At that time, Kensington also had few black faculty members. Consequently, it was not unusual that I was the only black student in my early American history class. Needless to say, I felt uncomfortable in that class, especially when the teacher discussed slavery.

Once, while the instructor was briefly going over the history of slavery in America, my worst nightmare came true. The professor began to show slides of the progression of blacks through slavery. I remember feeling all the normal feelings that most young blacks feel when they see pictures of slaves being beaten, whipped, and shackled to the bottom of a ship. I felt like a volcano ready to erupt.

He then showed a picture of Mammy, the well-known black stereotypical woman, whom we all know. She weighed about three-hundred pounds with charcoal black skin, large exaggerated red lips, and an old familiar smile on her face like she was happy being a slave. My professor said, "They depicted black women this way for several reasons. One reason was to ease the conscience of whites, who had slaves, and basically to show that blacks were happy being slaves. Whites also took away black women's sexuality and therefore depicted them as unattractive as possible in books and movies. However," the professor said, "many times they were reportedly raped by slave masters."

As soon as the professor completed his statement, a white student, my age, yelled out that the Mammy picture looked like my mama. Suddenly, everyone in the entire class began laughing loudly for what seemed like hours. I saw the person who said it. All that I could feel was rage. The volcano erupted. It took everyone, including the professor, to get me off the boy who talked about my mama.

Once they separated us, I grabbed my books and walked straight out of the classroom. I dropped the class, but still finished the semester at that school. I made up my mind, after that episode, that I wouldn't continue my education at Kensington University, or any other predominantly white college. That's why I'm at Norfolk State.

What a large dose of racism in the form of insensitivity and indoctrination—and it came from Morrison's professor and classmates. Morrison was so embarrassed and angry that he chose to leave the university and find a new one where he would feel more comfortable. Teachers with self-respect, black and white, need to be sensitive to their students. Negative matters should be talked about in a friendly manner. Trite matters, like the stereotyping of black women's appearance, should not be mentioned. Teaching is about more than preparing lessons and lectures. It's also about loving your students and possessing self-respect. When students feel loved, they learn. And they adore their teachers who have personal integrity and respect for all races in the classrooms.

And the story continues. Graduate professors can be as insensitive to black students as are high school teachers and college professors. Many black graduate students face racism daily. Many students spoke of being concerned about their grades. They often reported not receiving the grades they deserved, from elementary school to graduate school. One high school student told me, "When I got a B, I thought I deserved an A. When I got a C, I thought I deserved a B. I often thought that I deserved better grades than I received." Another student said, "The lowest grades that I should have gotten were As, Bs, and Cs. On homework, a white teacher gave me a D." My research, which I reported in an earlier book, showed that many white teachers deflate the actual grade black students deserved—and this in an era of grade inflation. In the majority of cases, while black high school students drop out of high school, in contrast, most blacks in colleges and graduate schools often accept the incorrect grades to ensure that they will graduate.[9]

Shirley is an exception. As doctoral students often do, she used to hang around the departmental office—to bond, trade news and gossip, and seek comfort. One day when Shirley was in the office, one of her favorite professors came in. They greeted each other and talked about their Christmas vacations. Only the secretary was there that day. Shirley asked if she could drop by his office and pick up her final paper. He said, "Yes. However, I can tell you your final grade in the course." Shirley replied, "That's even better." He said, "You made B+, the highest grade." Dismayed, Shirley countered, "Sir, I carried that class. I made perfect scores on all my work." He answered, "The other students got Bs. I graded you on the national level and the other students on the university level. You still made the highest score." Shirley's internal struggle caused her to blurt out, "Sir, black folks like their rewards just like white folks." He didn't seem to have a reply. Word circulated in the department that this conversation had taken place. Fortunately, the grade issue became a departmental joke, and the professor changed Shirley's grade to an A−. Shirley took a chance on derailing her doctoral studies. She was used to dealing with racist behavior, but she would not put up with racist grading.

WHAT TO DO ABOUT IT

In combating racism, children are our real hope. Children who never learn racism in the first place are the ones who will create a new society, one in which everyone is treated equally and fairly. Schools are one of the primary spots where children learn. The question is, Are they learning racism or are they learning fairness?

Furthermore, when black children start out being treated fairly at school, their confidence is bolstered early on, and they learn that they are as good as anyone else. Many black children, particularly those whose parents are educated, start out with good attitudes about school. Eager to learn, they sit up front, pay attention, and are ready to answer questions. They're well behaved. Unfortunately, their positive behavior doesn't always meet with a positive response. There are some well-meaning teachers, of course, committed to behaving fairly to all their students—but too often they are the exception rather than the rule.

When young children are ignored, insulted, and treated as second-class, they learn to feel bad about themselves. Their self-esteem plummets. Sometimes they act out in class simply to get the teacher to give them any attention at all, and a self-fulfilling prophecy has been created.

What White People Can Do

Schools have a great potential for demonstrating strong principles of fairness and justice. The principal sets the tone in a school, and a principal who is determined to see that all children are treated fairly will promote similar behavior among the school's teachers and other administrators. A principal who believes in justice puts that philosophy into action. Ignoring personal preferences and personalities, such a person focuses only on establishing social and academic justice in the halls and classrooms. He or she understands that all students need access to everything schools offer so they can reach their highest potential. To such a principal, the rights of all children are equally important.

School disciplinarians also play an important part in ensuring that black students are treated justly. It is up to them to ensure that corrections and punishments are handed out equally to everyone, black or white. The disciplinarian—often the assistant principal—is also responsible for ensuring that all other faculty follow the same guidelines. Fairness should be expected from all teachers, librarians, counselors, and other administrators. All children, regardless of race, need to be fully informed of what the rules are and of what behavior is expected. They need to know what behavior is not acceptable, and what the consequences will be if they break the rules.

Teachers play a crucial role in eradicating racism. Like principals and assistant principals, they can go a long way toward making every child's educational experience a fair and uplifting one. White teachers in particular are in a position to improve the learning experiences of black children. Not only do teachers need to grade every student by the same standards, they need to treat all the children alike—giving equal eye contact, paying equal attention. If some children are allowed to choose their own seats, then all children should have that choice. Children should not be allowed to reserve seats; they should be taken on a first-come-first-served basis. Otherwise, seating can become stark racism. Black students who raise their hands should be recognized and called on as readily as white children. They should receive equal amounts of praise and encouragement when they do good work. Their work should be equally displayed on bulletin boards and walls.

History teachers often play an especially crucial role in a black student's educational experience. Lessons about slavery need to be taught from a positive perspective. Too often, black students, from grade school to college, feel ashamed and embarrassed when the topic of slavery comes up. But why should they be ashamed? Neither they nor their ancestors were at fault in this tragic period of our history. Sensitive teachers will be aware of this potential reaction and take extra steps to reassure their black students. If fellow students make thoughtless and stereotypical comments about slaves, as happened in Morrison's history class, the teacher needs to immediately intervene. Unless a teacher qualifies these kinds of statements, they can burn into the mind of a black student, leaving a lasting scar. A good history teacher will find ways to help students of all races learn about and appreciate the many contributions, even acts of heroism, made by slaves.

History teachers should help their black students feel proud of their ancestors. Because of this country's history of racism, these lessons are even more effective when taught by white teachers. White teachers also have a powerful opportunity to inspire their black students to achieve and to help them believe they can achieve. Alford, from Illinois, talks in detail about Mr. King, a teacher who stood out in this way:

> I'm eighteen years old. I had this experience with my high school political science teacher, a thirty-year-old white man. He has had the greatest influence on my career. When I told him that my football coach had told me that the only way to go was to play football, he turned all that around for me.
>
> My teacher gave me what I needed to finish high school and to keep a hold on my dream. He gave me the encouragement that I needed and told me that everyone is the same, no matter what. "We all start out the same," he told me, "but it's what we choose to develop." I was choosing to develop my mind rather than my body.
>
> Without Mr. King to reinforce me, I could have been easily persuaded to play football and wouldn't have known any better. I want to challenge myself and let people know that I'll become somebody. At that time, the only dream that

I had was to become a lawyer. Without Mr. King, that dream would have been crushed by my white football coach. In a sense, Mr. King let my dream live on.

Dreams are the stuff success is made of, and Mr. King inspired Alford to dream. This story illustrates how sometimes it only takes one well-meaning white person to make a huge difference in the life of a black student.

Counselors also play an important role in the black educational experience. School counselors should encourage black students to follow their aptitudes and dreams. They should take time to talk with black students about their problems. Patrick, a twenty-year-old North Carolina student, talked about Mrs. Larnie, a white school counselor whom he loved. Mrs. Larnie made herself available to all students. When black students got in trouble, Mrs. Larnie was always there for them. She took the time to listen amiably to their problems and to offer solutions the same way she did for white students. She even invited a few black students to her home for tutoring. Unlike some of the teachers, Mrs. Larnie saw the good in the students. She made them aware of the fine qualities that they had never seen in themselves.

Coaches can play an equally important role. They can give qualified black players the same positions and opportunities to play sports as they give white players. Moreover, they can encourage academically oriented black players to pursue academics as well as—or even instead of—sports. Coaches often have great opportunities to befriend their young charges. Mr. Jolson, who was white, was this kind of coach, as Jameson, twenty-one, described:

When I was in junior college in Mississippi, I had a white football coach. I always turned to him when I had a problem. One time, when I didn't have a way to go home for spring break, I told my coach. And he bought me a bus ticket to go home. There's no better man than Mr. Jolson. I had a good time with my hometown family and friends and eating Mama's good food.

People like Mr. Jolson inspire us all. It is as if they light a candle on a hilltop and its rays illuminate the world. Again, one man made a difference in the life of a boy, a boy who was able to go home and eat his mother's good cooking.

What Black People Can Do

Blacks have their own work to do, both in and outside the classroom. As students, teachers, and parents, blacks also need to be well-intentioned, fair, and open-minded. What does it mean for blacks to be well-intentioned? It means they practice the same fairness and equality they expect from white people. It means they do everything they can to develop good relationships with the people around them and to behave in ways that promote equality and justice.

The home is where children learn these positive attitudes. Ideally, racism should be discussed routinely in black homes, so that children aren't afraid of it. Although many of us still battle racism daily, we cannot afford to let fear keep us from doing what we must to counter it. And there is much that we can do, all of us.

In many ways, middle-class black families are no different from their white counterparts. Dinner is typically the only meal the family sits down to together. Like other parents, black parents have to arrange schedules around part-time jobs, band practice, and other school activities. Dinner can provide an important opportunity for teaching children how to handle racism in the most positive way and for instilling attitudes of fairness and justice.

Concerned parents inquire about their children's day to find out details about the classroom, the playground, and so forth. Sadly, black children often have unkind acts, mean behavior, or other injustices to report. When this happens, it provides parents with an opportunity to help their children. Racism is perpetuated by black response as well as by the racist acts of white people. Well-intentioned black parents can help their children put the incident in perspective and guide them to find ways of handling the situation differently the next time. They can help their children realize that these incidents are not their children's fault and not something to be ashamed of. And they can encourage their children to take appropriate action, such as politely asking why when a teacher has marked a test unfairly or another student has been rude or insulting. Black children, unfortunately, do not lack for experience of racist school practices. Often they need parental guidance when the burden is too heavy for them to carry on their own. Sometimes it is helpful for parents to contact a teacher directly or to visit the school. Sometimes black children even feel the need to call their parents from school to tell them about what has happened to them, and parents should try to be available to their children in this event. Like most children, black children just want to get along with school personnel and with other children. Experience, however, teaches them to constantly be vigilant. This is a difficult burden to add to the learning process, for blacks of any age and parental support can go a long way toward relieving this burden.

Inside the classroom, black teachers, from kindergarten to graduate school, should be excellent. They need to know their subject matter, teach in great detail, impart an enormous amount of information, and teach or lecture in a congenial tone. Black teachers need to caringly maintain well-disciplined, orderly, warm, and loving classrooms. A teacher can be the boss and yet be on good terms with her students. I laughed at my jokes and my students' funny comments as easily as they did and had absolutely no problem restoring order.

Black students also have a responsibility. They should do their assignments. They should learn the course content. They should make As on all quizzes and tests. To complete the good experience, they need to respect and help their peers. They need to revere good teachers. When they encounter poor teachers, all students in a class should report them to school officials. Black students must learn to earn their rights collectively in black teachers' classrooms. The same response should be made to white teachers' incorrect class-room behavior, such as quoting black crime statistics and not white crime statistics in a criminal justice class. In this way, the American black student dilemma will come to a long-overdue end in the early part of the twenty-first century.

3

AT THE STORE

S hopping is viewed by most Americans as an enjoyable pastime, a pleasant way to get out of the house for a while and to contribute to the economy. Most of us cherish the opportunity to shop in cheery stores with congenial staffs. For most of the black college students I interviewed, however, shopping was not an enjoyable experience. In fact, they considered their encounters in stores to be among their worst experiences with racism.

PROBLEMS WITH OTHER SHOPPERS

Sometimes other customers were responsible for ruining those young people's shopping sprees. Casper, a nineteen-year-old student, told me about an experience he had when he was sixteen. His family had recently moved from the South to the Minneapolis–St. Paul area. His parents had given him and his brother money to shop for school clothes. A group of six teenagers, including Casper and his brother, went to the Mall of America to make their purchases. They were looking forward to a fun outing together. When they got to the mall, they were approached by a group of white teenagers who were about the same age as they were. The white boys started yelling racial slurs and throwing things at them. Casper and his friends decided to run.

Soon after that, the group of black youths encountered another group of white teenagers who seemed to be waiting for them. When Casper and his friends started downstairs on an escalator, the white boys began spitting on them. Casper was caught off guard. Since he was now in a northern city, and no longer in the South, he didn't expect these kinds of things to happen. Tears rolled down his face, and he felt hateful and vengeful. He never overcame the fact that he had been the victim of spitting—one of the most demeaning things one person can do to another.

By the time white boys become teenagers, they are prepared—as we have seen in the previous two chapters—to practice racism against their black peers. Sadly, black teenagers often don't defend themselves against whites because they are afraid of what the whites will do to them in return. Peer racism devastated Casper.

White adults are also responsible for more direct racist acts. Roycee, who was nineteen when we spoke, moved to Carlisle, Pennsylvania, when his father was stationed there. The family noticed only a few other black people in the area. Roycee decided to check out some of the local malls to see what they had to offer. When he got to the first store, he noticed that most of the people there, who were white, were staring at him. Soon he began noticing that the women were tightening their grip on their purses when they saw him. A few saw him coming and turned around to go in the opposite direction. Roycee couldn't believe this was happening in Pennsylvania—a northern city—in the 1990s. His mother couldn't believe it either. Roycee was so disgusted that it was difficult for him to wait for the school year to start—his school was predominantly black—so that he could stop feeling unwanted.

PROBLEMS WITH SALESPEOPLE

Essie, age twenty and from Virginia, was mistreated when she went shopping at a Great American Mall. At one point she sought service at a jewelry counter in a department store. The white saleswoman ignored Essie and instead helped the white women who approached the counter after her. Although she made sure the saleswoman saw her, the saleswoman didn't make any effort to offer assistance or even acknowledge her presence. Essie was infuriated by her obvious and potent act of prejudice. She finally interrupted the saleswoman and stated that she would no longer do business at her store.

These types of experiences with white salespeople were all too common among the students I talked with. Christi, twenty-one, had a similar experience in her Kentucky hometown. One day she visited a small, privately owned clothing store, where she began browsing and looking at some fairly high-priced merchandise. When she went to the counter to ask about the size of a particular dress, the white saleswoman, who was doing some paperwork, glanced out of the corner of her eye at Christi and mumbled, "Are you going to purchase that garment?" At that moment, a white customer approached the counter. The saleswoman stopped her work and immediately helped her. Christi's first reaction was to think, "I was here first." But instead of speaking up and risking a confrontation, she left the garment on the counter and walked out of the store. She felt mistreated by the saleswoman, and she was angry because she hadn't been able to buy the dress that she wanted. Essie and Christi's experiences illustrate the insensitivity and unfairness shown by white clerks to black customers across America.[1]

Young black shoppers sometimes feel completely invisible to white salespeople. June, twenty-six and a Virginia resident, and her black friend, Millie, for example, went to an exclusive clothing boutique in a southern city. The salespeople there were all busy helping their white customers. June and Millie looked around at the merchandise for quite a while. A salesperson never approached them. Finally, Millie told one of the saleswomen that she was an earring designer and was pleased to see some of her work on display there. When they found out who she was, the inattentive staff suddenly became extremely congenial.

Many white salespeople, once they spot black people at the counter waiting for help, often implement another common form of racism. "Who is next?" they ask, although who is next is clear to everyone—a black male or female. When a clerk asks who is next, many black shoppers have learned to state firmly "I am" to make certain they are served in the proper order. Flora, eighteen and from Massachusetts, clarified how this is done—although the practice doesn't always work, as in her case. She and her sister went to a store to purchase some cookies. When they went up to the counter, a woman was in front of them. Before the white saleswoman finished waiting on her, another white customer came to the counter. When the saleswoman finished helping the previous customer, she gave the white customer assistance. Flora immediately said, "Excuse me, we're next." Flora knew that saleswoman had seen them standing there. The saleswoman responded by wrinkling her face as if to say, "You can wait your turn." Instead of waiting, they walked out. Flora's story shows what a struggle it can be for young black college students even to buy cookies. Flora and her sister did what all thinking blacks do in these cases, when even speaking up doesn't work. They walked away, but without the cookies they had come to the store to purchase.

Even when it is successful, sometimes having to state firmly "I'm next" can bring regret. Emma, a nineteen-year-old Washington, D.C., resident, told me about going to a store to buy some shoes. When she arrived, the white saleswoman was helping a customer. No one else was waiting. When the sale was completed, two white women walked in, picked out some shoes, and told the saleswoman the size and color they wanted. The saleswoman started toward the back to get their shoes. Emma said, "I'm next." The saleswoman returned, and Emma told her what she wanted. Because she had corrected the saleswoman, Emma was able to buy the shoes she wanted. But later she regretted her purchase. She told herself, "The next time a white salesperson acts racist toward me, I won't buy the shoes. Nor will I spend my money anywhere a salesperson shows racism."

Being Watched

Salespeople not only destroy blacks' shopping experiences by ignoring them, they also do the opposite and turn on too much attention. Black males in particular often receive some form of unwanted attention when they walk into stores. Many of the young men I interviewed reported being asked, "May I help you?" as soon as they entered a store, while the white males there had not been asked this question. These students concluded variously that the purpose of this question was to put them on notice that they were being watched or to let them know that they had no business entering the store unless they intended to make a purchase.

Yet while their interpretations differed, all the students I spoke with took such behavior as a lack of respect. Even much younger people can sense lack of respect. Jason, now a twenty-year-old college student, experienced this kind of insensitivity when he was ten. Jason lived in a small suburb near Trenton, New Jersey. He used to go to the corner store down the street from his house, which was owned by an older white man. All the neighborhood kids—white and black—frequented this store to buy candy and snacks.

At some point Jason began to notice that the store owner treated him differently from the other kids. When white children entered the store, he laughed and joked with them. He asked about their baseball teams, school, and so forth. When Jason entered, however, the man would immediately ask, "What do you want?" Then he would watch Jason closely and tell him to hurry up and make his purchase. Yet when Jason went to the store with his mother or father, the owner treated him better than when Jason was alone. Although this man never directly made racial remarks, his behavior made it clear that he didn't trust young black boys.

Because Jason was only ten, it took him some time to realize that he was being treated differently. After he became aware of the owner's behavior, however, he decided to walk a couple of blocks farther to the next store. When he told his parents why he had stopped going to the other store, his father was ready to confront the owner. But Jason's mother didn't want to cause any trouble. She thought too much of herself to want to create more hurt and cause the memory of the incidents to linger. As a result, they never set foot in the store again.

The young women I spoke with also experienced the racism of being watched in stores. Lisa, twenty-one, told me about going to a mall in Norfolk, Virginia, where she was attending college. She went to a cosmetics counter in a particular store. She soon sensed that someone was watching her. Indeed, the saleswoman was watching her every move, but without ever asking, "May I help you?" Lisa left the store and purchased her items at another store in the mall. While exiting the mall, she passed through the first store. Once the saleswoman saw the packages in Lisa's arms, she immediately asked if she could help her. Lisa ignored her and left the store angry. It was painfully obvious that the saleswoman had not thought Lisa capable of buying anything until she saw her other packages.

Worse yet, the students were often both followed and watched. Velma, twenty-one and from West Virginia, noted, "The worst racist experience that I've ever had occurred while shopping in a white-owned and -operated retail store." The salesperson there had followed her around the store, watching every step she made and looking at every item she touched. Anna, thirty, whose hometown is in Georgia, reported a similar experience:

> I went to shop in one of the better clothing stores in a particular southern city. A white saleswoman followed me to see if I would steal merchandise. To avoid further annoyance, I bought a pair of earrings and left.

Many blacks realize they are followed because they are suspected of being thieves. Rosalyn, nineteen and from Virginia, was put off by a white saleswoman in a department store in Virginia, where she intended to browse and shop. When Rosalyn entered the store, the woman followed her everywhere. Finally Rosalyn turned around and said to her, "If you want to discover a thief, watch white people."

Many of these young black shoppers had seen white people stealing in stores. They realized that many white salespeople ignore the white potential shoplifters and instead concentrate on black youths, whom they suspect are only able to wear stylish clothes because they have stolen them—quite an unjust stereotype of blacks. The truth is that blacks don't steal any more than whites do. To believe otherwise, and to act accordingly, is pure racism.

Velma also described a painful experience of being suspected as a shoplifter. She was twenty years old and home on summer vacation from college. One day she went to a small boutique to browse. While there, she was followed throughout the store by salespeople. As Velma was leaving, a saleswoman stopped her and asked her to turn out her pockets and to empty her purse. When the saleswoman realized she had made a mistake, she simply explained that some merchandise was missing from the store. Velma was humiliated by the salesperson's automatic assumption that since she was black she must be a shoplifter.

Incredibly, whites not only follow black youthful shoppers; they also trail black employees. Mamie had this experience:

> I was nineteen years old and worked in a store that employed a white female security officer. For some reason, she felt she needed to follow me. I was an employee, and there was no need to follow me. I assumed she thought that I would allow blacks to steal or that I would steal money from the cash register. Finally, I confronted her. Initially, she was embarrassed, but then she denied her behavior.

Sometimes even when whites employ young blacks, they can't bring themselves to trust them, which is unfortunate. The truth is that most black youths want to make a good impression on white supervisors. They work hard and make sure that no one steals merchandise under their protection—blacks or whites.

"How Are You Going to Pay for That?"

Of course there are many white store owners and salespeople who do not believe that blacks are the major perpetrators of shoplifting. But many people do seem to believe that blacks do not have the means to buy nice things for themselves. This prejudice can unfortunately compel some black youngsters to either shoplift—as they're suspected of doing anyway—or to waste a salesperson's time by trying on more expensive items only to purchase a cheaper item with less commission value.

For example, one time Morrison was shopping for a leather jacket. The salesperson asked him if he needed help. He answered no, but the salesperson didn't move away. Morrison moved to a different part of the store. In a mirror, he saw that the salesperson had followed him and was watching everything that he did. Morrison started walking in circles just to make sure that he wasn't being paranoid. He walked to the front of the store, then turned around and went to the back of the store—and there was the salesperson. Morrison asked him, "What do you want?" The salesperson asked, "What are you talking about?" Morrison responded, "Why are you following me?" The salesperson looked away, but didn't move. Morrison told him to have a nice day.

Then Morrison told the salesperson's manager that he had been ready to spend $500 on a jacket, in cash, but that his salesperson (he called him "I Spy") had ruined his shopping experience. He then took out his wallet and showed the manager that he had the money. The manager and the salesperson stood there dumbstruck. They apparently could not imagine that a young black person could have that kind of money. Morrison nicely summed up the black experience of shopping: White salespeople can ruin it.

Many college men and women described having their buying power underestimated as characteristic of their shopping experiences.

For example, one Labor Day weekend, twenty-one-year-old Nathaniel from South Carolina and his friends stopped at a national-chain convenience store. Several young black males were milling about the store. While Nathaniel was getting a carton of beer, a white cashier came to him and said, "I told your kind of people that we don't take food stamps for beer and that you need proper identification." Nathaniel ignored her, but she repeated herself, so he cursed her. He hated the notion that the saleswoman assumed that all blacks are on welfare, that they are unable to pay for what they want on their own.

Nathaniel went on to reflect on corporate welfare. He wondered how many whites had become wealthy through government bailouts—railroad owners, automobile manufacturers, even jet manufacturers. In contrast, blacks (and many more whites) who are on welfare only get a monthly pittance that covers the expenses of one week out of every month. There is absolutely no comparison between the huge amount of welfare that wealthy whites receive and what poor blacks receive. Assuming that all blacks (or all blacks who buy beer) are on welfare is not only racist, but it also demonstrates real ignorance of how things really work in America.

The students described various ways of reacting to these types of experiences, which left them feeling inferior, hurt, and angry. Nathaniel was left feeling so angry and disempowered that he ended up cursing at the saleswoman who had insulted him. In some cases, they left the stores and never returned, as did Morrison when he tried to buy a leather jacket.

Lonnie, twenty-six, related this experience:

It was about time to go shopping for school clothes. My brothers and I were shopping in Williamsburg, and we had seen some interesting figurines. We realized that we were in a white store with expensive items. The salespeople watched us constantly, implying that we might steal or break something. We started walking around in the store and picking up several figurines. They ranged in price from $150 to $10,000. When we picked up an item, a salesperson would ask, "How much does it cost?" and "How are you going to pay for that?" This happened three times. We continued to tell the salespeople that we didn't need any help. Yet, they kept bothering us. We walked out of the store.

In this case, even obviously middle-class black youngsters weren't given a chance to educate themselves about the merchandise in the store. Lonnie and his brothers were simply curious about the figurines and wanted to learn about them. They used the only way they thought was available. While white youngsters might have also been watched, since the figurines were costly, they almost certainly would not have been quizzed about their spending capabilities, as these boys had been.

In other cases, the young men and women bought expensive items, paying beyond their means to prove that they had buying power. Vernon, twenty-seven and from New York, described having done this:

It was Christmas and I was shopping for a present to give to my girlfriend. I wanted to buy her a Coach purse. I went to a large department store in New York City. Because I was going to meet her at the health club to play racquetball afterward, I was dressed in sweats. I noticed that the salespeople were staring at me as I walked through the women's clothing section on the way to the purses. I was approached by a saleswoman at the Coach counter, who asked if I needed assistance. I explained that I was shopping for my girlfriend and had decided to buy her a Coach purse. She started helping me make the selection, showing me all the smaller bags, which were priced relatively low. My girlfriend wanted a larger bag, which I explained to the saleswoman. She hurriedly picked out a few for me to choose from. She explained that all of the larger purses were between $200 and $300. I paused for a second and took a deep breath. I quickly made the decision to select a $300 purse and put it on my charge account. The saleswoman had prejudged me according to my appearance. I was angry, but not shocked. I later wrote a complaint letter to the manager, who in turn sent me a formal apology and a gift certificate.

Young blacks need to fight racism whenever they can. But when they fight it with their pocketbooks, they hurt themselves twice as much. Vernon should have bought the $200 purse. He didn't because his pride was—understandably—hurt. However, writing a letter afterward showed that Vernon didn't mean to take his mistreatment lying down.

The black college women, like Mary, who was twenty-three and lived in Ohio, with whom I spoke had similar experiences to relate:

On my twenty-first birthday, my boyfriend and I were in Ohio and went to a jewelry store. He had decided to buy me a deluxe watch. When we entered the jewelry store, there were only white employees. The white saleswoman didn't ask whether we needed assistance. After waiting twenty minutes, I asked her to show us some watches. It took about an hour to select the watch I liked. By that time, the saleswoman didn't think we were serious about buying. Consequently, she began trying to brush us off. When I asked how much the watch cost, she replied, in a smart way, "$600, and there are no cash refunds." When my boyfriend paid cash for the watch and insurance coverage, the saleswoman was surprised and speechless. It is a shame that white people feel that blacks can't afford expensive things. It upsets me. But at least my boyfriend was able to purchase the watch and to prove we had money.

Mary showed that several types of racism can be operating in one shopping experience—being ignored, not being taken seriously, then being treated as if her boyfriend couldn't afford expensive items. Young blacks want to feel good about themselves. They want other people, especially whites, to realize that they too are able to be prosperous. They face enormous internal difficulty when they are confronted like Mary was. Mary's only vindication was that her boyfriend was able to show a lot of cash—money that in this case he fortunately could afford to spend—and impress the racist saleswoman. It goes without saying that it shouldn't take that kind of demonstration to be treated with respect.

Doris, twenty-two, also had a story to tell about experiencing several different types of racist behavior at the same time in a boutique and how she chose to fight back:

When I was seventeen years old, my cousin and I went to shop in Lawrence's Boutique, on Fifth Avenue, in New York City. The boutique was owned by whites. Inside the store, the salespeople acted as though we were not there. This treatment lasted nearly half an hour. A white customer and her two daughters entered the boutique. A saleswoman rushed to them and offered assistance. While we looked at merchandise, another saleswoman watched us relentlessly. Once she was convinced that we were not stealing, she approached us and said, without us having inquired, "I am sorry, but we don't have a layaway plan." That unsolicited statement upset me greatly. She attempted to make it seem that blacks can't afford expensive purchases. The saleswoman forced me to prove that I could afford to shop at that boutique. I selected several items and charged them on my American Express card.

After the entire selection of merchandise was approved, I told the saleswoman that I no longer wanted the items. I should add that it was a lengthy process to credit the merchandise to my charge card. I wanted to give her a difficult time. And I wanted her to know that blacks can afford expensive items. That's what racism makes one do. She could've made a nice profit for the store. Instead, she made racist remarks. I'll never give that store our business.

Doris fought a good fight against racism in the boutique. She was able to make life difficult for the saleswoman, giving her the opportunity to experience the shock of her racist assumptions. Even though the salesperson struggled with processing the returns, Doris's struggle was greater—the anger borne of racism was rekindled in her heart, and she was deprived of the things she desired.

Racism even followed several young women to the bridal shop. Janice, twenty-four and from Ohio, had this story to tell of being mistreated while shopping for a wedding gown, what should be a joyful experience, and how she fought back:

Even though I am young and in college, I am also married. Before my wedding, I went to a bridal boutique to buy my wedding dress. When I asked about a dress I liked, the white saleswoman told me, "The clothes in our boutique are expensive. Perhaps you need to go to an outlet shop to purchase your wedding dress." Because I was dressed in a jogging suit, I believe she thought I was a low-budget woman on welfare. I had simply walked into a boutique, approached a white saleswoman, and questioned her about a particular dress. She had looked down on me. I was upset. I don't understand why white people are going forward instead of backward in their cruelty. After she prejudged me, I bought the wedding dress, returned it to the store, and reported the incident to the Better Business Bureau.

White salespeople need to learn that youngsters who are dressed casually can still come from affluent families. When Janice encountered the saleswoman's prejudice, she fought back by buying the wedding dress she desired. But her internal struggle was so great that the only way she could feel satisfied was to return the merchandise and get a refund. Yet again, hers wasn't a complete victory—she still did not end up with the wedding dress she had really wanted.

WHEN THE POLICE GET INVOLVED

One would think these stories about encountering racism while shopping are as bad as it gets. But it gets worse. Many young people reported situations in which false suspicions or accusations ended with the police or security guards becoming needlessly involved. Calvin, twenty-two and from New York, told me about his experience:

> I went shopping at what used to be one of my favorite stores. I set my bags on the floor to free my hands to sort through clothes in my size. Before I could get halfway through a stack of polo shirts, two white guys came out of nowhere and jacked me up while the third guy dumped my things on the floor. White people were looking at me as if to say, "It figures. A black man is stealing." I've never been so humiliated in my life. They went through all my things but couldn't find any stolen items. Then they explained why everything happened so fast and why I had been handcuffed. The reason they gave for placing handcuffs on me was for their safety. That is, they said, "Because of past experiences, we wanted to guarantee our safety."

Amanda, twenty, described an equally painful situation:

> My brother, his friend, my sister, and I were in a store, located near several colleges in Boston, Massachusetts. We looked around in the store but didn't buy anything. We left, and my sister drove down the street. In a matter of minutes, a police

officer signaled us to the side of the street and searched the car for goods that someone had stolen from the store. When he didn't find any stolen goods from that store or any other store, he released us. However, after searching the car, he searched my sister. Consequently, when the police officer left, she drove back to the store and questioned the salesperson. The white saleswoman said that she didn't know about the incident. Nevertheless, my sister eventually sued the store. As a result, the saleswoman was fired, and we were awarded a monetary apology.

Police officers saw fit to search innocent citizens who had done nothing more than look around in a store. Being searched, because it is so personal, is a particularly humiliating form of racism. Amanda and her sister fought back by going to court and receiving some compensation for being innocent targets of racism.

Black women are targeted as well as men. In Atlantic City, Lila also was subjected to a search:

Once I went to Atlantic City with my parents. After we went in one store, my parents left. I stayed to continue shopping. While I was still looking around, a black man came over to me. He pointed to the white manager and said, "He asked me to search you." I allowed the search, which proved useless. When the search ended, the black man looked ashamed and gave me a warm smile.[2]

Leona, twenty-two and from North Carolina, also described being searched:

One time my family members and I were falsely accused of shoplifting because of the color of our skin. My fifteen-year-old sister, my seventeen-year-old cousin, and I (I was twenty) were browsing in a clothing store. Three police officers rushed into the store, grabbed our bags, and searched us, as well as our bags, without saying a word. Following the search, the police officers said they had received a call that three young ladies were stealing. The store and police officers embarrassed us and didn't offer an apology. Because we are black, they were suspicious of us.

These searches are clearly the outgrowth of the stereotype that all blacks (and only blacks) steal. Audrey, twenty-three, shared her experience:

I was nineteen years old and living in Pennsylvania, when this situation occurred. I entered a department store. I happened to be browsing in an aisle where a white woman was stealing merchandise. The manager, who was white, told me to come to her office. When she determined that I hadn't stolen merchandise, she only apologized for the mix-up.

Anthony, twenty-three, was also accused of stealing. He was in a local convenience store in his hometown, Henderson, North Carolina. About one minute before he entered the store, someone left with a case of beer hidden under his coat. Anthony related what happened next:

When I entered the store, the white salesman was upset. About that time, police officers arrived. The salesperson told them that I was the one whom they saw stealing the beer. He said that I was wearing a long overcoat and a pair of jeans. I had on sandals and shorts with a T-shirt. It couldn't have been me. Yet he was determined to make me the thief. When the salesman began describing me to the police, they knew that I was not the one. First of all, I couldn't have changed my clothes that quickly. Second, he kept changing the story to make the person be me. The police officers tried to be patient, but finally they told the salesman that he had the wrong man. The man shouted out, "Who cares? You know they all look alike anyway."

The salesperson gave voice to an all-too-common stereotype—that all blacks look alike. It hardly needs to be stated that there is no race or ethnic group in which the people look alike. And if all blacks look alike to whites, then how can they be trusted to correctly identify perpetrators? Essentially, the salesman didn't care that he had made a false accusation, indicating that as long as a black person was punished, justice had been done. That is, in the logic of prejudice, all blacks are guilty of one crime or another anyway.

The college women I spoke with also experienced this kind of stereotyping. Lillian, thirty, related this incident:

On July 23, 1993, I turned twenty years old. I visited my aunt in Oceanside, California. For my birthday present, she planned shopping and beauty-parlor outings at our favorite mall. When we arrived at the beauty parlor, my aunt selected a white hairdresser, who told her they didn't do our type of hair. After a brief confrontation, we decided to leave because it seemed they had already judged us the minute we entered the salon. At first I was angry and refused to take no for an answer. Suddenly, I realized it was my birthday and that it was not worth trying to make white people understand that in many cases, such as ours, black people's hair is the same or a better grade than whites. Therefore, we left without further altercation.

Lillian didn't put up a fight because she did not want to expend the energy it would take on her birthday. She also intimated that white people are slow learners. My view is that white people have had a long time to learn and reinforce racist stereotypes, and they don't want to stop the behaviors that make them feel superior.

WHAT TO DO ABOUT IT

Shopping has become a favorite American pastime. We enjoy looking for things that we think will add to the quality of our lives. We
enjoy getting out of the house and spending time with friends at the
mall. But for black people, as we have seen, it can be a bittersweet
experience. White people enjoy a freedom to shop not always
extended to blacks. But this situation can be improved.

What White People Can Do

Salespeople are central to any shopping experience. They can make
it pleasurable for the customer, or they can make it unpleasant,
even demeaning. White salespeople need to offer the same help and
services to blacks as they do to others—from respectful treatment
to courteous assistance.

For example, when shoppers want merely to browse, they
should be allowed to do so. This means that salespeople should not
hover under the pretense of rearranging merchandise. All customers appreciate being acknowledged when they enter the store
and asked if they need assistance. If they are "just shopping," then
salespeople need to let them browse at their leisure.

If customers—white or black—are ready for or seeking assistance, then salespersons should show them the merchandise they're
interested in, including different sizes, colors, or styles. Can they
afford such an expensive item? Why not assume that they can—
rather than that they cannot, if they are black. All salespeople
know what constitutes good service, because they receive such service when they are shopping. Smart salespeople can imagine how it
would feel to be denied this.

At store counters, shoppers should always be taken in the order
of their arrival. Salespeople should never wait on white customers
first, while black customers are waiting, almost invisibly. All shoppers, regardless of skin color, should be treated with fairness and
respect.

On a subtler level, white salespeople need to watch how they hand receipts, bags of purchases, and change to shoppers. Many salespeople will hand these things to white customers, but they seem afraid to touch a black person's hand, even briefly or accidentally, so they put the receipt or change on the counter. A subtle behavior? Yes, but racism operates on all levels. How easy it would be to do things differently—to look people in the eye, to smile, to hand them their receipt. Countering racism consists of addressing such differences in treatment, detail by detail.

My appeal to both salespeople and owners is not just moral— it's also financial. Treating customers well brings in more business, while treating them badly sends them away. People speak to their friends and neighbors, reporting their shopping experiences, positive and negative. Why not bring back all your customers—black or white? White business people may not fully appreciate how rare and wonderful a simple thank you can be to a person who has been accustomed all his or her life to rude treatment. While it is a sad commentary on racism today that such small gestures can be such a thrill to a black shopper, at the same time, it can be so easy to provide them.

How can we as a society create these upright, uplifting salespeople? Some white people grow up with good intentions, raised in families that value fairness and equality. Others learn in school, if they see teachers and administrators modeling fair and just behavior. Employers bear the responsibility of providing appropriate on-the-job training for employees who haven't received it before. Companies can hold customer-service training sessions that emphasize the value of every customer, including blacks. Managers should insist on friendly, fair, and respectful behavior toward everyone who enters their stores.

Other shoppers can also help in such training. Whenever a salesperson ignores a black shopper but then asks, "Who's next?" as whites approach, those approaching can speak up by saying something like "I think that this person was ahead of me" or "These customers have been waiting for your attention." A word to the manager might prove beneficial for the salesperson's education as well. Whatever is done, it should model good manners.

Good manners are contagious. When one person starts being polite, helpful, and cheerful, people around them start behaving the same way. White customers can be friendly in dressing rooms, smiling at black customers or paying someone trying on a new dress in front of a mirror a compliment. Small gracious words and gestures make a big difference. If many white people were to take such small steps toward treating everyone equally, then racism would start to abate.

What Black People Can Do

Black salespeople also need to treat everyone equally and with respect. They have their part to play in making every shopping experience pleasant and enjoyable for their customers.

Black customers should be patient and polite, both to the salespeople and to other customers. Being rude back to a rude clerk doesn't make anything better. By demonstrating dignified good manners, black shoppers can offer an example for other people to follow. They too can wait their turn politely, say please and thank you, and do all they can to encourage good behavior in return.

After all, shopping is a group experience. It takes people of all colors—shoppers and browsers, clerks and managers—to make it a pleasant experience for everyone. An important aspect of shopping is that it offers a relatively safe and neutral place for whites and blacks to encounter each other. For those who have never interacted with people of different races, shopping can be a good place to start. When the shopping experience is good, that positive experience in turn spills over into other areas of life—the workplace, the neighborhood, schools, churches, airports, entertainment venues, and so forth. Since so much is rooted in ignorance and fear of the unknown, familiarity is one of the best ways to get rid of fear.

Getting to know one another better, even in small ways, can have long-term positive effects on our society. If we can meet as equals at cash registers and in check-out lines, we can go on to meet as equals everywhere we go. And that's the way it should be.

4

IN THE
WORKPLACE

any young college students in my study found getting a job—both during the summer and during the school year—to be quite difficult. Some said that it was while job hunting that they had their worst encounters with racism. Unfortunately, discrimination in the workplace is nothing new, and many of the young blacks I spoke with focused their discussion on the problems they had with hiring officials. According to journalist Lynn Walker, hiring officials discriminate against blacks by using test results to purposely place job applicants in the unqualified category. Feagin and Feagin found that hiring officials use "aptitude or intelligence tests, without proving their relationship to predicting job performance."[1]

These practices help to explain why, for example, a majority of black women have "found their way into clerical and service jobs." Because black women earn less than all other workers, it is clear that this procedure serves to exploit them as an abundant, cheap source of labor.[2] Another way that hiring officials keep blacks from getting jobs is by hiring whites and paying them higher wages. This practice causes blacks to bear the heaviest burden of unemployment and to experience the greatest deprivation in every sector of the economy. As a result, a majority of black women are either unemployed or work in low-paying jobs.[3]

For a book that I wrote in the mid 1980s, I conducted a study of 240 African American women in southeast Virginia who had not been able to get jobs. All these women, while pursuing job openings, were either denied an application or told that they were unqualified or that there were no openings.[4] In the late 1990s I am hearing many of the same stories. The college students in my study related again and again their experiences with being denied jobs, receiving low wages, racist treatment, racist stereotypes, racial slurs, failure to get earned promotions, and job punishment for excellence.

"THAT JOB HAS ALREADY BEEN FILLED"

Tyrell, nineteen, shared with me a typical story of being turned away from a job. He knew that a particular store in South Carolina was hiring in an area in which he had plenty of experience. When he went to the store, the manager told him they were no longer hiring. Less than a week later, the manager hired a white male.

Job discrimination starts early. While Clarke, who was twenty-two when we spoke, was a senior in high school and searching for a job in various stores in a small town in Georgia, he was consistently denied a job. Clarke and his friend spent about two weeks going back and forth between different retail stores in search of a part-time job. Clarke's friend was white. Clarke had known him about two years, and they were considered close. The boys focused their efforts on a certain department store because they knew it was hiring. After their interviews, they went home together and hung out as usual. The next day Clarke's friend telephoned to say that he had gotten the job. Clarke was happy for him and knew that he would do well. He never took the difference in their race into consideration when he wondered why he had not been hired as well. Two days later, Clarke's friend came by his house and told him that he had quit his job that day. Clarke was surprised that he had quit because it had taken so long to get the job. Then his friend explained. The manager, a white woman, had stated that she needed another cashier but didn't want to hire anybody black because blacks were always stealing. Clarke's friend told her that he knew a black guy who doesn't steal. She replied that she had been in the business a long time and that black people were always trying to "get over" in one way or another.

After hearing what the manager had said to his friend, Clarke felt ashamed—not because he had done anything wrong, but because someone had made assumptions about him based only on his skin color. This manager didn't know him from the next black man, but then because she was racist, she didn't need to know him—just "his kind." Clarke felt angry at her and at the national corporation that hired her for allowing this type of individual to determine who was eligible for a job.

Lucerne, twenty and from Virginia, had a similar story to tell. Lucerne had two years of experience in retail work and was looking for a job. When she found one that matched her qualifications, she requested an application form. The hiring official hesitated before handing it to her. Lucerne completed the form and returned it to her. Even though there were no customers in the store, the manager told Lucerne that she didn't have time to look at it and that she should telephone later.

Lucerne called back a few days later. The manager told Lucerne that the position had been filled. Yet the Help Needed sign was still in the window. Lucerne asked a white friend to inquire about the job. The friend reported that she was told they were still hiring.

RECEIVING UNFAIR WAGES

Although some white hiring officials let a few blacks into their places of employment, these black youths are often offered lower wages than whites with the same training and experience. Some white employers find ways to get around laws specifying wages. The students need the money and will work for less than whites receive. They are also afraid to report and confront the owner. Any confrontation could result in loss of job, which would hinder the students' goals.

Since it is still true that equally qualified and experienced women are often paid less than men, black women suffer a double disadvantage in the workplace. For example, Callie, twenty-six, told us, "There are discrepancies in salaries of experienced white females and black females. I've seen black women earn $10,000 a year. With the same qualifications for the same job, white women earn $12,000 annually."

Mattie, twenty-two, told me about this painful situation, which involved not only being underpaid but also working in an unfriendly environment:

> I worked for two years in a government building in Washington, D.C. My high school had obtained the job for me. From day one, I experienced racism. For four months, my supervisor, who was white, barely spoke to me. Every day he passed my desk without saying a word. His secretary was also white. It was my job to help her. Instead of helping, I began doing all her work. All the tasks the supervisor assigned, she gave to me. This continued until one day he asked her to do something while he stood at her desk. She didn't understand how to perform the task; consequently, she asked me to do it. He told her that he had given her the assignment numerous times and that she had always completed it. Then he asked, "Why, all of a sudden, have you forgotten how to do it?" I told him the truth. Three weeks later, she was terminated, and a black woman was hired. That was the first day that he and I had ever spoken.

Mattie's story is the story of many working blacks. The students often reported that their white colleagues fail to initiate conversations or even to say good morning—a simple courtesy. The unfriendliness in the office resulted from a kind of routine racism that whites practice against blacks. It was also a consequence of old patterns of white employer-employee relations. But the second part of Mattie's story is also all too common. Too many black youngsters—and adults—are assigned lower-ranking jobs with lower salaries and then given work that belongs to a higher-ranking and higher-paid person—without proper recompense, of course.

NOT GETTING PROMOTED

Along with exploiting black youngsters for cheap labor, many whites expect their black employees to work either without receiving promotions or without receiving them on time. Most people need incentives to work. Fair and timely promotions and comparable wages are two of the best ways to inspire blacks to work. Blacks are tired of working and still living meagerly while making whites financially comfortable. They want the same work incentives that whites desire.

Sadie's story is a good example of how some corporations treat young blacks. One summer Sadie, forty-one and a Virginia resident, got a job at a telephone company. When she took an entry-level exam, she scored higher than anyone else in her office. She consistently volunteered to work more hours than scheduled. At the end of each day, her supervisor always congratulated her for her good work.

Three months later, a job became available in another office, and it paid $200 a week more than her entry-level job. Because she had gotten the highest score in her office on the entry exam, she applied for the job and was by far the most qualified applicant. But Sadie's supervisor denied her the position and instead gave it to a white woman whose score on the entry exam was less than half of Sadie's. Sadie was angry about her supervisor's decision, so she confronted her. The supervisor couldn't give a concrete reason for denying Sadie the position, so Sadie reported it to her second-level supervisor. That supervisor removed the white woman from the position and gave it to Sadie.

Sadie's experience is typical of the experiences reported by the college students in my study. To get deserved promotions often required a confrontation of some sort. Sadie had laid the foundation for her promotion in every possible way. It shouldn't have been necessary to go over her supervisor's head. Sadie was lucky. She had a fair-minded second-level supervisor. In so many of the other students' cases, going over their supervisor's head didn't pay off—the second manager proved to be just as racist as the first. Among other things, what these managers need to realize is that high productivity at work comes from a fair work environment—including fair promotions.

Some supervisors refuse even to discuss promotions with black employees, who are forced to continue in their jobs without advancing for years. This situation exists everywhere, from corporate America to the farmlands. Vernon related his experience:

> When I was twenty-three years old (I'm still in my twenties), I worked for a company, and my immediate supervisor would not communicate with me about promotions. Whenever I asked him about promotion criteria, he talked in general terms. His responses were always negative. He didn't recommend minorities for promotions. I think that he would hate to see a minority advance in the company. I reacted negatively to this situation. I would get smart, not speak, and refuse to make eye contact with my supervisor. I saw white men and white women with less seniority move twice as fast as me.

Vernon's experience is fairly universal. As the students experienced it, many whites seem to dislike seeing qualified blacks move ahead in the workplace. When they had less seniority, white managers used that as an excuse to not promote them. When they had more seniority, it didn't seem to count.

Many black youths reported being promised a promotion by their white supervisors and then being disappointed when it didn't come through. Fred, a twenty-one-year-old California resident, for example, worked as a bagger at a grocery store, and his supervisor suggested that he was in line for a promotion. After he had worked at the store for a year, his manager told him that she thought he was ready to work at a cash register. The next day, however, when Fred got to work, he was told that he would do better bagging and they didn't need him to work at a cash register after all. Needless to say, that was a big letdown for Fred.

WHEN WHITES GET BETTER TREATMENT

Another form of racism practiced by white managers is blatantly treating their white employees better than their black employees. Celestine's summer experience is typical. She was nineteen when we spoke and a Virginia resident. For several days she worked as a cook at a pizza restaurant from five P.M. until closing. At closing, the manager always counted the money and Celestine and the two waitresses cleaned up. Then the waitresses left after they washed the dishes. Celestine felt that everybody should stay until the cleaning was completed. The waitresses felt that they should wash only plates and that Celestine should wash the pots and pans and other utensils and mop the floor. Often after Celestine mopped the floor, they dropped food on it so that she would have to mop it again. Celestine used to stand for eight or nine hours daily without a break. She felt that it was her job. Celestine said, "Although I was quite pissed, I never argued with the girls or supervisor." She knew that confrontations often double the hurt of racism. One dose is difficult enough. Double doses of racism have been known to cause sickness, especially high blood pressure. Smart blacks don't work themselves into a frenzy with whites. It's better to recognize what one sees in the person—a sense of inadequacy.

Marsha, nineteen and from Virginia, also described a similar experience at her job. While she was working in a white-owned grocery store with two other blacks and four whites, the store owner always assigned the black employees tasks that required them to work inside a freezer as well as in other hazardous and undesirable places. He required that Marsha and the other black employees sweep and mop the floors nightly while the white employees took care of the cash register and wiped counters. The good jobs were never rotated.

After three or four weeks, Marsha asked the supervisor why their duties were different from those assigned to the white employees. The supervisor replied, "You're inexperienced." Yet he assigned the same jobs to the newly hired whites as he did to the more experienced whites. Although Marsha and the other blacks needed the money, they quit their jobs and convinced their families to stop patronizing the business.[5]

In a perverse twist, even when black employees are treated somewhat well themselves, they are expected to treat other blacks poorly. For example, some white employers not only give their white customers better treatment than their black customers, but they also expect their black employees to follow suit. At the age of nineteen, Russell received his first job as a salesperson in a store in Manhattan that sold fine men's clothing. Every day his boss would talk to him about black customers. He told Russell, for example, "Black men who come into the store don't know the color, style, designer, and price of clothing they desire. It's a waste of time to give them a great deal of attention. When white customers come into the store, be just the opposite."

Russell was glad for the job, but he soon saw a connection between how he was treated his first day at work and how black customers were treated. That day, Russell had dressed nicely for the occasion—a white shirt, a paisley tie, khaki slacks, and black loafers. His supervisor went in the back room and got a ladder. He told Russell to change the air filters in all the air conditioners in the store. When Russell began changing them, the supervisor purposely turned on the air conditioner to blow dust and dirt on his clothes. His clothes and face became covered. When he got down off the ladder, his supervisor patted him on the back and laughed.

Russell recollected himself by going to the restroom to wash his face and hair and to find the strength to make it through the rest of the day without further humiliation or injury. Actually, he never quite overcame his humiliation. Other salesmen had been watching, and further, they were never asked to do such menial tasks or used as the butt of practical jokes. Russell pretended to be strong and overlooked the negative and concentrated more on the positive. He told himself that this was just a summer job and that he would be returning to Norfolk State University that fall. Yet he was told so many negative things about black men that he started feeling inferior to whites. As a result, he quit the job before the summer break ended.

BLATANT STEREOTYPES

As we've seen before from so many students' stories, stereotyping is an all-too-common form of white racism, and it exists at the workplace just like everywhere else. Leona, who worked on a stock replenishment team for a nationwide chain department store, experienced a typical form of blatant stereotyping, namely, the presumption that all blacks steal. Fewer blacks than whites worked on the team. Unlike with the whites, the supervisors watched Leona and the other blacks continuously to determine whether they were stealing merchandise. Because of continued losses, the supervisor laid Leona off; the other black employees were fired.

The claim that Leona was stealing could not be proved, so she was recalled to work. She appreciated how many white employees were on her side. Yet she continued to be treated differently. For example, they were careful about what they said around her. Leona continued to be watched, while white female employees stole shoes, purses, and much more. Leona said, "I wanted to let them know how I felt, but I was afraid I would lose my job."

Leona realized that when stealing is involved, then white supervisors follow the stereotype and automatically put the blame on black employees, even if it means laying them off or firing them for no good reason. The young people felt that their white supervisors should either trust them as much as their white employees or that they should watch everyone equally.

Melissa, twenty-one and from Virginia, also described how she experienced stereotyping at the workplace:

> As soon as I began working at my job, I experienced whites' stereotypical behavior. My experience began when I told a black co-worker about my dream. The dream concerned two men who broke into my house and robbed me. While I was telling the dream, my white supervisor was standing nearby. After I had finished telling my dream, my supervisor bluntly announced to me that the men in my dream must have been black.
>
> For a moment, I lost my cool. I forgot where I was and asked him, "Does it matter what color they were or what happened? All white people are the same. You all think that blacks are the only ones who commit crimes. You fail to realize that whites have been stealing since the beginning of time. Whites stole this land from the Indians and stole us from our native land. You white jackasses have been stealing all along. That's why you think we steal. It's your nature to steal. By the way, the men in my dream were white and looked just like you." Since that incident, I've never said another word to him.

Melissa felt that her supervisor was projecting his own nature onto black people, and she attributed his racist behavior to this projection. She openly countered his stereotype about blacks stealing, but probably only to confirm another blatant stereotype, namely, that blacks get uppity about race. Melissa neither quit her job nor was she fired. Yet the racist incident had put her in an uncomfortable position at her job.

RACIAL SLURS

Sometimes young blacks experience stereotypes interwoven with countless other forms of racism—especially racial slurs. Marcus, a twenty-eight-year-old New York resident, had this experience while working on Wall Street:

> The worst racist experience that I've ever had occurred at the national stock exchange. I was twenty-three years old. It began in August 1989 and lasted until I resigned in August 1992. I was the only black from my firm working on the trading floor. Actually, I was a stock clerk on the trading floor and a data entry operator at my firm. I knew my jobs quite well. However, my knowledge of my different responsibilities caused me to get promotions and therefore less respect from my counterparts, since they were envious of my knowledge and implementation of job assignments. My co-workers often discussed their prestigious backgrounds, including their Ivy-League colleges, their neighborhoods, and their parents' occupations. Also, I was the only black in my department at my firm. The worst thing that happened to me was being called "boy" by a broker in the trading pit. I pretended not to hear him. Consequently, he repeated himself not once, not even twice. He seemed to say it a hundred times. All I could hear was "boy, boy, boy."
>
> I felt about four feet high as I walked toward the restroom with tears in my eyes. I sat in total chaos and wondered whether I should confront the white broker or go over his head and tell someone with authority, such as the senior vice president at my firm. It took about two weeks before I decided to

report him. Before I had reported him, the broker's comment was, "If it makes you feel any better, I have a black girlfriend in Trinidad." I didn't respond. Actually I felt worse, because it seemed as though he was saying that black is second to white and that he was willing to date someone who is considered less than a white female. There was something about the statement that just didn't seem correct to me. On top of the ignorance of his character, he never attempted to apologize for having done wrong. The vice president and the manager, on the other hand, were concerned and respectful toward me as a human being and a dedicated employee.

I believe that my entire racist experience at the stock exchange was a scheme the brokers used to prohibit me from getting promoted, or, should I say, receiving my just due. One day my manager called me at home and asked if I would come in early to show him and my senior vice president how to balance the brokers' accounts and operate the SIAC data line. This is a direct line that we have with Chicago and other stock exchanges, including COMEX, NYFE, and NASDAQ. I later found out through a reliable source how valuable I was to the company's success, but somehow I wasn't using this bargaining power to my advantage. Nevertheless, whenever the company hired someone, who was always a white man or woman, I was assigned to train and introduce the new member to the brokers (our customers) on the trading floor. Somehow the new employees gained more respect on the floor during the first week than I had gained in three years.

The brokers gave the new guy season tickets to see the New York Mets and New York Yankees play baseball, took them out for drinks on Fridays, and conversed with them daily. My reaction to this favoritism caused me many headaches, depression, and insecurity. I was hurt, excluded from certain affairs and not respected as a black man by most of the brokers on Wall Street. I knew that to overcome the dilemma, I must resign early in the game or cope with the problem until I was willing and able to leave. My family and older friends were understanding and supportive in helping me make a positive change. The result is that eight months later, I'm finally getting the opportunity to tell my story of racist corporate America.

Marcus details some of the racism that he faced on Wall Street. His supervisors took advantage of him by using his knowledge without compensating him adequately. The brokers treated new-comers kindly while treating Marcus badly. The worst example of their bad treatment was calling Marcus "boy" on the trading floor. Because of its historical and cultural baggage, blacks understand-ably hate this term. Slaves were called boy by their owners. During segregation, whites often called grown black men boy, and today, as we've seen, whites still call young black adults boy when they want to keep them down.

Calling a black person "colored" is as old and prevalent a slur as calling a black male boy. For decades blacks have not identified their ethnic group as colored. Yet, amazingly, many of the students in my study told me about white people they encountered who have never learned either to pronounce the word *Negro* correctly or to call them by the right title.

For example, during the summer of 1993, Farley, twenty-four, worked at a warehouse in Ohio with predominantly white male employees. These employees called blacks "black guys" or "colored people." Farley didn't approach them because of possible conse-quences, but the name calling made him angry.

Susie, also twenty-four, was subjected to such epithets in her own home:

My work supervisor was casually discussing in my home that people are all the same. That she had no problem with "coloreds." In some manner or another, in the midst of the conversation, my supervisor referred to me as colored. I was shocked and angry. Then I asked my work supervisor to refer to me by name rather than as a colored. The experience took place in my home, located in the state of Kansas. I am a counselor and believe that my supervisor referred to me and other blacks as coloreds because of ignorance and a belief in stereotypes about blacks. Because I'm not even twenty-five years old, I was not born when whites called blacks coloreds.

Susie wasn't even born when blacks were regularly called coloreds by white people—her white supervisor taught her the term. Some whites apparently don't want blacks to forget the racism they have perpetrated.

Ellen, twenty-one and from North Carolina, related a story concerning another long-standing racial slur:

While I was working in a store, a young white male attempted to make a purchase with his mother's credit card. I was required to obtain approval from my manager. The young male commented on not being trusted by "you people." Before he left, I tried to engage him in a discussion of the meaning of this comment. My effort was in vain.

The episode was particularly frustrating for Ellen because the young white man would not engage her in a discussion of why he made a racial slur. Sadly, like too many others, he did not feel the need to take responsibility for his racist actions.

As we have seen in previous chapters, whites can easily degrade young blacks by referring to them as nigger, even at the workplace. Lawrence, a twenty-one-year-old college student, worked at a well-known store in southern Virginia. One day when the telephone rang, he picked it up and said, "Hello, M. N. Jack. May I help you?" There was no response. Consequently, he repeated himself. In the background at work he heard somebody say, "That must have been that nigger who answered the telephone." Lawrence asked his

white co-worker, "What did you say?" His co-worker, who had
made the remark, didn't say anything, but he asked to speak to one
of the managers. There was nothing done about it.

Such racial slurs know no class lines. Jennie, twenty-three and
from Virginia, related a white girl's comment about better-off blacks:

> I worked for a nationally known motel chain with a white
> co-worker, Lisa. We cleaned rooms. One day Lisa observed a
> black family leaving a room in the motel. We had cleaned
> several messy rooms before entering this one. Lisa said, "This
> is our last room." Then she said, "Niggers always leave their
> rooms torn up." Before she could get the words out, I looked
> in her face to determine whether she realized that she had just
> called those blacks "niggers" in front of me. Then she looked
> away strangely and said, "I'm sorry. I didn't mean to say it like
> that." I inquired, "How did you mean to say it?" She didn't
> answer. Before that incident, she and I had been friends. We
> sometimes ate lunch together and were together after working
> hours. After this incident, it was all over. She tried to apolo-
> gize, but it was unnecessary, because she had already shown
> me what she was all about. It made me angry because, if it
> hadn't slipped out, I realize that I would've never known she
> felt that way about blacks.

Jennie's experience shows how a white person doing a menial job
can still express condescension toward black people, even blacks
who would likely be considered of a higher class—after all, the
white cleaning woman was cleaning up after them.

Kitty related this story about being called a nigger—by the very
person she was helping:

> In 1988, I was sixteen years old and employed in a nursing
> center for the elderly. I worked as a dietary aid, and it was my
> duty to help nurses feed clients. While I was making a cup of

coffee for a white client, who happened to be blind, she asked me, "Are you the little nigger girl?" I told her, "No. I am Kitty, a black girl," and walked away from her table.

This young student didn't understand why an elderly woman, whom she was helping, would call her such names.

Clayton, a twenty-six-year-old from North Carolina, experienced yet another ugly slur:

On a particular occasion, a young white naval officer was assigned to my department and discovered that he was in charge of an all-black crew. He turned to his white friend and said, "Look at all these ignorant sons of bitches." Needless to say, we young men were shocked and immediately reported him to his senior officer. He was punished and demoted as well as removed from important duties.

Some racial slurs are more subtle, serving to demonstrate underlying stereotypes about black people. Jim described his experience as a construction worker:

At my current age, twenty, I went to work at a construction site in Trenton, New Jersey. My father got me the job. That is his line of work. The job required that I work with several people. Everyone, except a white guy, seemed compatible. This guy was about twenty-seven years old. Whenever I asked a question, he put me down. He even asked me, "Did you learn anything in school, or did you just hang around?" At first, I ignored his questions, because I thought that he would soon stop asking them and making smart remarks. I was wrong. On Monday mornings, he would ask, "Who did you rob over the weekend?" I began retaliating and letting him know what was on my mind. After thinking it over, I realized that I wasn't acting smart. If I lowered my level to his, I would just be giving in to his perceptions. I decided to go about it a different way. I worked extra hard and came in earlier, took short breaks, and put my best in every job. After a while, people started noticing how hard I was working. Now I am guaranteed a job every summer. The racist joker never tried to make peace with me, but he stopped his comments and ignorant attitudes toward me.

Jim, like many others I spoke with, opted to handle racism in the workplace by demonstrating excellence on the job. Although this approach doesn't always work, sometimes, as with Jim, it clearly does.

Charlene, twenty-one years old and from Virginia, experienced another kind of racial slur at her job in a fast-food restaurant:

This racist experience with a white person really frustrated me. I work at a nationally known fast-food restaurant. I receive people's money and give them change. All the employees in this restaurant are black. Once a white man came into the restaurant and placed an order. When I gave him the total, I held out my hand to receive the money. He looked at me as if I had done something wrong and threw the money on the counter. I picked it up and attempted to put the change in his hand. Instead, he said, "Put my change on the counter because I don't touch people like you." I put his change on the counter. Then I retaliated. I said, "Why do my people have to cook your food?"

Young people working in stores often endured racist customers. When Walton was twenty years old, he worked as a cashier in a grocery store in Virginia. One day the store was crowded, and all the lines were full, except his. When he offered to take customers in his line, hardly anyone moved from the crowded lines. They just looked at him. Walton said, "I felt like I was diseased and had an empty feeling inside."

Mitch, a bagger in a well-known grocery store, had a similar story to relate:

When I was twenty years old I worked at a grocery store in Chesapeake, Virginia. I was a bagger and asked a white customer if she wanted her groceries bagged in a paper or plastic bag. She said, "I'll bag my own groceries, because your hands are dirty." This made me feel inhuman, shocked, and angry. I overcame the situation by focusing on the good experience that I had with whites.

Arlethia, a twenty-nine-year-old Virginia resident, gave this personal example of the racism that can occur even at federal jobs:

I was working in the mail room at a United States post office. The manager was standing in a certain location. I was standing near him. He told me, "You do not belong on my side of the floor, old black gal." I had never been called a name because of the color of my skin. When it occurred at a United States post office, I felt that I had been pushed back one hundred years. He had told me to stand there and wait for the mail. I was told that I could file a formal complaint, but I didn't.

WHEN BLACKS DO THEIR JOBS TOO WELL

Another extremely prevalent form of racism found in the workplace today is mistreatment of blacks who excel at their jobs. The students I interviewed spoke variously of resistance to their expertise, being penalized for job excellence, interference with their performance, and altercations when their performance exceeded that of white employees. Marie, nineteen, spoke about her experience working at a mall:

One day I reported to work at a store in a Virginia mall and was the only person on duty in the women's department. A woman telephoned, asked me to hold a particular dress, and told me that she would pick it up later in the day. I put the dress aside.

When she came to our department, I was helping a customer. In the meantime, she walked around and browsed. After the other customers left, I asked if I could help her. She said, "No. I talked to a saleswoman earlier on the telephone." I said, "Oh, you spoke with me. You requested this dress." I held up the dress.

The first thing that she said was, "I wasn't expecting you to be black. You sounded so intelligent on the telephone." I stood there in shock. Then I went from shock to anger. I told her, "Perhaps you should return to the store tomorrow, because I don't think that I'm intelligent enough to ring up your dress on the cash register." She became upset, obtained my manager's name, and left the store without the dress. My manager never mentioned the incident.

Marie experienced a white customer's stereotype that blacks aren't intelligent. The customer also indicated that she didn't expect blacks to excel in the workplace, another stereotype. Blacks often work harder and more efficiently than some whites, while earning less.

Sheral, twenty-three, related this experience:

While working in a U.S. navy facility, I experienced problems with a white female co-worker. She neither respected nor acted in a professional way toward me. The problem was that she viewed my position as superior to hers. Consequently, she would not work cooperatively with me. This resulted in a mutual negative attitude that we had toward each other. I was in a position that required me to check figures. If I received inaccurate information, she was required to correct it in the computer. We were always working under deadline pressure. On one occasion, I asked that she correct the information in the computer and give me a report. She told me, "When you tell me to, I'm not going to correct a damn thing." This response upset and angered me. I sat down to cool off. She passed by my desk. Out of anger, I slapped her face. After looking shocked, she didn't do anything but continued walking. Only three people in the office saw what happened. After returning from the bathroom, she asked what information I needed corrected. After that incident, I didn't have any more trouble getting needed details corrected in the computer. Unfortunately, it had taken my rage to get results. We compromised. I also realized that the best time to obtain her assistance was when we both had deadlines to meet.

Some blacks feel they have to go to dangerous extremes to counter white resistance in the workplace. Sheral was fortunate that her actions didn't cost her job.

Peaches, twenty-six, experienced resistance to black job excellence in a public library:

I was twenty-one years old and worked in a library in Virginia. I had just received a promotion from library aide to library assistant. Shortly thereafter, the administration transferred me from the main library to a small branch library. The branch library was patronized mainly by elderly whites who didn't want a young intelligent black woman working there. These patrons had been spoiled by white librarians. In fact, the only thing they wanted a young black woman to do for them was keep the building clean. I could be the only one at the desk, and they (male and female) asked, "Will you get me some help?" When they asked me to find help, I didn't say a word. I looked to the left and right, back at them, and asked, "May I help you?" Realizing they didn't have any other choice, they told me what they needed. I should also say that the only other black person who had ever worked at that branch library was a janitor.

As a result of her experience, Peaches felt penalized for being good at her job. She went on to describe what happened next:

> I was twenty-four years old and still working at the branch library. When a white librarian was hired, my life changed. Because he was a librarian, and I was an assistant, he was my superior. There was one other assistant. Since I had seniority, if he had questions, he asked me. But he couldn't simply ask the question. He would say, "I have a question for the expert." That bothered me. I felt like he was punishing me for my experience and knowledge. He continued this behavior for two months. At the end of this period, I decided to put an end to it. The only reason that he stopped saying, "I have a question for the expert," is because I refused to answer him. Unless he asked me the question without using the word *expert*, I ignored him.
>
> On one occasion, I responded by saying, "Go find an expert and ask her" and walked away. Of course, subsequently I was considered as having an attitude problem. The issue was resolved because he realized that if he wanted answers to his questions he had to speak to me in appropriate and non-offensive language. In my opinion, the situation began because the black library director told him that if he had any questions about the library, he should ask me.

The male librarian was so envious of Peaches' knowledge that he actually turned it into a joke. She had to do what so many working blacks do—put him in his place. Fortunately, it worked for Peaches. Sometimes doing this results in loss of employment.

Many white employers greatly dislike it when their black employees outperform their white employees. Genie, twenty-two and from New Jersey, told this story:

> I was employed at a jewelry store that used sales quotas to determine salaries. I was the top salesperson. The assistant

manager was angry because my sales figures were higher than his. He wanted to be the center of attention, but because I was, he couldn't gain that status. Consequently, one day he called me a "black female dog." I was totally shocked. I reported him to my regional manager and kept doing my job. The manager talked with him. After that our relations were never good, but at least they were tolerable.

Genie's experience underscores the creativity of racism. It's not relegated to employers; it's also found among upper management. Another common practice is clear in this story. Instead of whites applauding blacks' success, they become jealous. Their inferior feeling influences them to try to raise their status and to lower blacks'. A healthier society can be created in this new century by mutual encouragement between whites and blacks and by applauding excellence—all excellence.

Antoine, a twenty-four-year-old Illinois resident and former marine, told me his worst story about what happened when he did excellent work:

While I was serving in Operation Desert Storm in 1990, my squad was selected to have a news team follow the course of each day. My captain said that it was to show the American public that their tax dollars were being spent wisely and to show that the war was winnable. The captain told us that our squad was selected by him and our first lieutenant because we were the most experienced and most professional combined anti-attack team (CAT) in the Persian Gulf.

While most Marine Corp units were packing their gear and saying good-bye to their families, my unit weapon's company, the Third Marines, had already been in Iraq for three months. We considered ourselves the salt of Operation Desert Shield, and we could prove it. I studied maps of the desert and led my squad on many patrols until my squad and I knew the desert like the back of our hands, especially the sand that stretched from Saudi Arabia to Kuwait. Anyone who has spent time in the desert knows that trying to navigate there is like trying to navigate at sea. Everything looks the same.

During the time that my squad was navigating the desert, it was twice as dangerous. More than a few marine squads found themselves wandering into one of the many minefields that Saddam Hussein laid out especially for those marines who were forward and careless. Thus, my squad was very proud to be selected. We bragged and boasted to the other squads. I was especially proud because I was the squad leader. After I heard that we were selected, I strutted around camp all day with my chest stuck out. Later that day, it began to sink into my brain that out of all the CAT squads in Third Marines, my squad was seen as the best. Just three years before, I was just another poor black teenager from the projects of Chicago. No one even looked at me.

I called home and told everyone from family to friends that I was going to be on television. They said that they would watch to see me. The day that the news reporters showed up at our camp, my squad was standing tall and at attention in front of the entrance to the camp with highly spit-shined boots that we had stayed up all night polishing and with our best set of camouflaged utilities. We knew that we looked good. There stood eight white marines in column formation with one black marine (me) standing out front. I had arranged us this way, so that it would be absolutely clear that I was in charge.

The civilian reporter, escorted by his cameraman and my lieutenant, walked right up to my face and said, in a sort of sissy voice, "You've got to be kidding me. You will never do. We want someone more like apple pie, like the boy next door. We want the American people to believe their son could be here risking it all for our country." It was at that very moment that he turned to a white member of my squad and told him to stand in my spot and to act as though he was the squad leader.

I looked to my squad and my lieutenant for support, but they wouldn't say anything. All I heard was silence. I not only felt betrayed, but I felt like a fool. I felt betrayed because I taught those young marines everything they knew about CAT and navigation. My lieutenant was the one who had helped promote me to squad leader in the first place. He told me that I was the best corporal he had and that he was promoting me for that reason and for that reason only. He made it seem as though we were beyond color at the Third Marines.

I felt like a fool. I had actually believed that garbage they say in television commercials and in brochures. For example, they say that the Marines are neither black nor white, that they are all one big green machine with marching brothers until the end. I thought to myself, what a joke that saying is. I withdrew into a shell for almost the rest of my tour in the desert. I told myself, "To hell with the big green machine. I'm getting out. I'm going back to college to achieve something. No one can take away my education." At the time, I was only twenty-one years old.

The students made clear that earning money often led to encountering the most hurtful behavior. To add insult to injury, there was very little that many of them could do about the insulting behavior. It's so amazing that some whites practice racism all the time and anyplace. It is my hope that this book will awaken them to the plight of blacks and encourage them to stop being racist. Just one glimpse of our plight, I believe, will be enough to get many whites to change. I hope the stories in this book provide that glimpse.

WHAT TO DO ABOUT IT

Countering racism at work is of paramount importance. Having to face racism on the job influences everything from ability to perform to advancement opportunities. We all want to earn a good income and to advance in our jobs. Blacks are perhaps more eager to avoid racist treatment in the workplace than in other places. Like everyone else, they want to fit in, do well, and move up the ladder.

But before one can fit in, one has to *get* in. Many jobs are filled without communitywide postings. We've all heard about the "old boys' network." In recent years, there's even been an increasingly influential "old girls' network" on the rise. Often blacks miss out on well-paying jobs because they are not connected to these networks that would enable them to learn about openings days or weeks before postings and know exactly what sort of applicant the company is seeking, how the company operates its business, and so forth. Usually neither the "old boys" nor the "old girls" are connected to black networks. However, a few blacks are being hired in high-profile jobs. They are doing well because of their skills, knowledge, and friendship with insiders. More blacks—both young and old—must assume a humble posture and make friends on the job. It will pay off.

What White People Can Do

White employers are in a position to help qualified blacks find employment and receive fair salaries. Fair employment policies without regard to race are a must. Many businesses have training programs. Blacks should be informed and white employers should be fair in their admissions. A qualified black should never be denied while a less qualified white is admitted. And poorly prepared but capable blacks should be given a chance to learn and to advance. Black students at every level of education need to be given an opportunity to receive the training necessary for them to get good jobs.

Once blacks are hired, there are still hurdles. Say a predominantly white company has an opening. Somehow a black person discovers this fact, applies for the position, and is hired. Now the hard work is just beginning. Every employee needs to learn the lay of the land—about the turf battles, the uneasy truces, and other unseen problems. The new black employee needs this information even more than other new employees—but he or she will often find that it is harder to get. What new black employees need most is someone who will help them find out who's who, what the unwritten rules are, who has power and influence. Without this knowledge, new black employees can inadvertently cause problems for themselves by stepping on unseen land mines. Once so injured, they can be hindered in their progress and success.

Well-intentioned white managers and employees can provide access to valuable information when it comes to office politics and inside information. They can coach and encourage, give advice, share expertise. They can also open doors, include their black colleagues in special projects, recommend them for advanced training, and model fair, just behavior toward them for the rest of the work force to emulate. Mentoring black colleagues or employees is especially helpful. Supervisors and managers can take an interest in young black men and women and guide them as they move up their chosen professional ladder. Each company has its own culture—its ways of doing things—and no matter how well-educated a person is when they enter the workplace, they still require guidance about the company climate. These are the things a white mentor can offer to younger staff members.

Good relations with colleagues of all skin colors make work more enjoyable as well. Johnson, twenty-one and from Massachusetts, describes how this works:

> My best experience with whites was when I was employed in a grocery store located in a predominantly white town. When the people came to shop, they didn't act racist. They greeted me with a smile. My fellow co-workers were nice. They helped me learn how to use the cash register, bag, stock, and open and close the store. Most important, the head manager became my friend. He knew that I needed money to attend school. He arranged for me to get two raises during that summer. The

manager and I attended three baseball games together and ate together after work and games. He was really nice. I could trust him. I hated to leave, but it was time for me to return to school. I left with an evaluation and a leave of absence to return during the holidays and the following summer.

Johnson demonstrates the give-and-take required to build a good work relationship. When people are young and inexperienced, they need to be humble enough to accept training and to let other people teach them what they know. Johnson could have been defensive, unwilling to listen to advice. He could have resisted people's efforts to help him learn. Instead, he welcomed and benefited from it. The whole town benefited as well, because people learn good behavior by observing it in others. On the part of his co-workers and neighbors, their friendly behavior is a classic way for whites to end racism. A few whites began a ripple effect that changed the whole town. I believe that there are enough well-intentioned whites to start a ripple effect that could change our whole country.

Every workplace offers the opportunity to develop meaningful relationships between blacks and whites. Judy, thirty-four and from Virginia, told a heart-warming story about finding a job. Judy was a graduating senior from the Massachusetts Institute of Technology and had majored in business. Following the tradition of graduating seniors, she went to the M.I.T. alumni office and began reading the alumni directory. She decided that she wanted to locate in Atlanta. To her delight, she found a fellow alumnus who was white and a CEO at a megacorporation in Atlanta. She sent him her curriculum vitae and a letter asking for his assistance with employment in his company.

When he received her package, he simply wrote on her application, "Handle this." His secretary sent it through the proper channels. The personnel office knew what the comment intended. In a few days, she received a call and was asked to visit the corporation, at their expense, for an interview. Within a week, she received a contract. Judy was ecstatic. Her fellow alumnus never inquired about her race. The only thing that mattered was that she was an alumna at M.I.T. Judy was given a highly responsible job. One mistake would cost the corporation thousands of dollars. Judy handled the job impeccably. Needless to say, Judy's wages matched her great responsibility. Soon after she got the job, she sent the CEO a thank you letter, and later they had a pleasant meeting.

Judy's fellow M.I.T. alumnus set the pattern for every white CEO, supervisor, and professor—male and female—for eradicating racism in hiring and employment. He provided a model for improving the status of a long oppressed people—a people who did the back-breaking work to build white businesses. The beginning of this twenty-first century is a good time to multiply Judy's experience too many times to count.

Jeffrey, twenty-four and a resident of Delaware, told us about his good experience in the military:

> My navy commander was the only white person who has had faith in me. He listened to me and respected what I had to say. He watched over me while I was in the navy. I confided in him one day that I wanted to attend college. The commander could see that I had a lot of potential and didn't want to deny me an education. When my commander got promoted, he used the proper procedure to make sure that I could fulfill my dreams. He made sure that I was released from the navy with an honorable discharge. Then I had time to attend college full-time and secure my future. As a result, I am a sophomore at Norfolk State University with a 3.4 grade point average.

Jeffrey's navy commander epitomizes the ideal of a military officer—morally upright, committed to excellence and integrity, and willing to take action to further those beliefs. He made a huge positive difference in this young man's life. He could just as easily have let Jeffrey down, dismissed his dreams, discouraged him from having goals or trying to succeed. This officer is a perfect example of the big difference just one person can make in a young black person's life. As we've seen, it's not only the officers and supervisors that influence the workplace. Peers and colleagues can also be of vital assistance to blacks.

What Black People Can Do

Blacks have their own responsibilities when it comes to creating a fair and equal workplace. Certainly, they want to be treated fairly when it comes to wages, promotions, and other job opportunities. In turn, they need to behave in ways that match these desires—just as other employees do, no matter what color. Black employees should take their work seriously and perform their duties responsibly and professionally, even if their job seems unimportant or is entry level. Good employees look for ways to expand their job responsibilities rather than stubbornly saying "that's not my job" when someone asks them to do something. They do what any good employee needs to do: be quiet, be on time, be neat, dress appropriately, be professional, be reliable and dependable, and do good work.

Businesses thrive when co-workers have good relations with one another. Part of what makes a good employee is being friendly, honest, willing to offer assistance as well as to accept it. Colleagues should take an interest in one another's hobbies, families, and concerns, without, of course, taking away from getting their jobs done.

Black employees would do well to identify as quickly as possible with one or more white people at work who seem to be fair-minded and well-intentioned. By cultivating these people as friends, colleagues, supporters, and even mentors, black employees can improve their work experience in many ways.

As we saw in Johnson's story above, being a good colleague is of course a two-way street, just as any relationship is. The black employee needs to maintain an open mind and be willing to learn. Black employees, especially young adults just starting out, need to be open to constructive advice and guidance. Even modest demurs by whites need to be probed for specifics. For example, if a supervisor says, "Your work is good enough," instead of "Your work is excellent," then the black worker needs to ask questions about what keeps his or her work from being better. When criticism comes— and often it will—then it's time for the black employee to seek out white associates to garner advice for getting back on track. Well-intentioned white people can and do provide access and insight. Blacks should try to get over the frustration or anger and accept help when it's offered.

Studies show that a paycheck alone does not create job satisfaction. This is as true for blacks as it is for whites. Blacks, like anyone else, enjoy being paid well for the work they do, but they also want to be appreciated, recognized, and respected. They want to do work that matters to them, that develops their talents and satisfies their creative potential. Like anyone else, black workers want to feel that the world is a little bit better because of what they do. They want to take pride in their work.

As our society evolves, more and more blacks will find themselves in positions of responsibility and influence, supervising others, making management decisions. They have a role to play here as well in the effort to counter racism. They too can become mentors to young black people just starting out. They can encourage them, advise them, help them over the pitfalls. They can also influence white supervisors they work with, showing by their example how to treat everyone fairly and justly. By their own behavior, they can demonstrate that blacks can be valuable, valued, and successful people in the workplace—and everywhere else.

Although these are lofty goals, they should be easy for everyone to realize. Black Americans, however, have a particularly daunting task because they need to do these things despite the racist behaviors they encounter. They know how discouraging it is to work hard, to do one's best, to produce excellent results and to still be passed over for promotion. It's encouraging to note that already many of the blacks I interviewed have learned how to rise above such challenges. Ignoring the ignorant, cruel behavior of others, they live up to their own personal standards of excellence. The example they set should be an inspiration to us all.

5

BLACKS AND LAW
ENFORCEMENT

Historically, blacks have been unfairly treated by law enforcement officers. As late as the 1960s, in Newport News, Virginia, white police officers arrested blacks walking down the streets staggering because they had high blood pressure. Arrests are only the beginning of the problem. I have sat in courtrooms on Monday mornings to listen to cases. The police officers and defendants always had different stories, and the judges usually ruled in favor of the arresting officer. I knew that some of those rulings were unfair and that many blacks were unjustly fined and imprisoned.

Although the military justice system is less likely to convict blacks than the civilian legal system, the military court system is still rampant with racism. You recall that in 1994 I did research at Fort Leavenworth, Kansas. The colonel on the base and all the military personnel assigned to my project were excellent. I was investigating military legal justice. I found that military justices are supposed to follow written sentencing rules. With a strong background in the formal structure of arrests and sentencing in the military, I did in-depth interviews with black, white, and Hispanic military prisoners. They told me that blacks were sentenced to more years than whites and Hispanics for the same crimes. Some white males told me they were sentenced to Fort Leavenworth for five years for a particular crime, but blacks were sentenced to ten years for the same crime. The point I am making here is that even in our best judicial system, black males are given sentences that are twice as long or longer than others for the same crimes.

Police officers, both civilian and military, are supposed to protect citizens. It is not their duty to arrest unfairly or to present information inaccurately so that judges sentence unfairly. It is clear that police officers and judges—civilian and military—follow their own informal codes of law, codes that are dangerous to black America.

In my interviews with young middle-class college students, I found that even the mention of law enforcement in America hits a raw nerve among them. Essentially, young black people's experiences with the police are much different from white people's. The college men especially related how their encounters with the police began in elementary school and have not yet stopped. The following stories demonstrate the relationship between black college men and women and white police officers and security officers. These stories all serve to portray the struggle that law enforcement puts in the hearts of the young, gifted, and black.

Edward and William, whose fuller stories we will hear later, both had something to say about the resignation and helplessness they feel in the face of this pervasive problem. Edward, nineteen and from Washington, D.C., stated simply:

> We knew that, without reason, except that we were black and driving a luxury automobile, we were treated like criminals. That was in Virginia. I felt resentment, but I decided that it wasn't the first time and that it probably wouldn't be the last time. After all, I'm a young black man.

William, twenty and a Delaware resident, added this observation:

To be honest, I really don't know what I can do to prevent this type of unjust treatment. The law even breaks the law. The difference is that they get away with it.

A majority of the students I interviewed told me about being stopped by the police while sitting in their cars, driving down streets and highways, and walking in neighborhoods—even their own. While outside the safe confines of their homes or dormitories, these students underwent whatever treatment was deemed appropriate by the police officers they encountered—treatment that was often unpleasant and unnecessary. Most of the young people reported most fearing being stopped and searched.

BEING STOPPED

Most of the students reported that they began being stopped by the police when they were still fairly young, even before they got to college. Monica, twenty-one, was stopped when she was a high school student in her school uniform riding with other young black people:

When I was sixteen, my cousin, a friend, and I, dressed in our school uniforms, were on our way to school in Boston, my hometown. We were pulled over by four police officers. Two officers were riding in one patrol car, and two other officers were in a second patrol car. My father drove by and saw us. He stopped, got out of his car, and attempted to see what was wrong. One officer told him, "Don't come over to this car." After receiving a ticket, we continued on to school. At first, we laughed about the incident. With more thought, my cousin, my friend, and I became angry. We realized what it meant to be black in a New England city in America; we realized what it meant to be black in a white community; but most importantly, we learned how difficult it is for whites to accept educated blacks.

The same thing happens in all parts of America, not just in New England. Lawrence, a twenty-year-old resident of Massachusetts, related his experience in a predominantly white town:

> While a male friend and I were riding through Pungo, Virginia, we were stopped by police officers. They asked, "Why are you in Pungo?" My friend, who had been driving, asked the officer why he had stopped us and whether we were speeding. The officer replied, "You were not speeding." My friend asked the officer again, "Why did you stop us?" The officer responded, "Because you're young black kids looking for trouble." In keeping with my friend's personality, he cursed the officer and drove off. Fortunately, the officer didn't attempt to follow us, but the situation made us upset and uncomfortable.

This officer's racism was blatant. He admitted that the reason he had stopped these black youths was their skin color. If you're young and black, even if you're a college student, you must be out looking for trouble, or so the belief goes.

Sometimes, of course, blacks are guilty of breaking the law. But even when this is the case, they almost always receive more severe treatment than whites in similar situations do. Thirty-three-year-old Briding's experience was typical of the reports of many black women:

> I was driving down a street in Jacksonville, North Carolina, in 1985. I was scheduled to be at the bus station by five P.M.; however, the heavy traffic made me late. I decided to take a shortcut. That's when I ran a yellow light. At the same time or perhaps seconds later, a young white girl turned down the same street. She, too, ran the same yellow light. The officer signaled me to pull over and waved the white girl on. When the officer walked up to my car, he shouted, "Are you blind?

That was a yellow light that you drove through." I said, "No I'm not blind. I saw it, but I need to be at the bus station by five o'clock. I'm sorry." He replied, "Sorry didn't break the law. You broke it." I responded, "I'm sorry that you didn't get the car behind me. Its driver broke the same law." He became red in the face and said, "I didn't see her. I saw you." I asked, "Officer, how can you say that? That car was behind me, and you were behind it. As a matter of fact, I made it my business to write down her license plate number. If I have to, I will hire a lawyer and fight you and the courts of North Carolina with everything I've got." I pulled out my pen, looked at his badge, and began writing down his identification. Before I finished, he said, "That won't be necessary. But you get out of town. Niggers should learn how to obey the law."

This officer's racism was also blatant. But Briding was in no mood to accept a ticket. She proceeded to get his identification to equalize the situation.

BEING SEARCHED

It was typical for young black males driving nice cars to be stopped and then searched. Indeed, I never heard a single case in which this did not occur. Thomas, thirty-two and living in an upscale neighborhood in Virginia, had firsthand experience with this type of racism:

During 1991, when I was thirty, while in Virginia Beach, Virginia, traveling home late one night in my BMW Series, I met up with a Virginia Beach police officer. No sooner than we had driven past each other, I noticed the cop had done a U-turn. He followed me for five miles until I turned into my driveway. Then he flashed his blue lights on me. He asked me to get out of my car. My neighborhood was 85 percent white.

I told him that I lived here, and he said, "Don't smart off to me, boy." I raised my voice, insisting that he ring the door-bell and inquire. My wife must've heard my car drive up and seen the car lights while peeping out the door to see why I hadn't come in the house. At this time, the officer asked her if she knew me. She replied, "Yes, he's my husband" and asked "What's wrong?" At that point, he permitted me to enter my residence. Bear in mind that I was a thirty-year-old navy offi-cer in uniform returning home from my ship after a long day on board. The officer never said, "I'm sorry," nor did he offer an explanation for his actions. Obviously, I asked for his badge and squad car number to file a grievance early the next morning. We received a letter of apology from the chief of police and a copy of the incident report of wrongdoing that had been placed in the officer's permanent service jacket.

Even driving a BMW, claiming residence in an upscale neighbor-hood, and wearing a military uniform didn't make Thomas immune to racist policing. Sadly, blacks are more prone to being searched while driving new cars or while in upscale neighborhoods. Many whites have not learned that blacks want and deserve the same things that whites do.

Although more black men than women are stopped and searched by the police, I did speak with some young black women who had some stories to tell. Eudora, twenty, recalled that while she was driving on the highway in Norfolk, Virginia, with some friends, a white police officer signaled to her to pull over. He frisked the pas-sengers, searched the car, and asked to see Eudora's driver's license. He told her that it was Easter weekend, and that police officers were searching cars to make sure people weren't transporting drugs from Virginia to New York. The officer didn't find any drugs. But what had made Eudora a suspect? Her skin color.

It seems that some white police officers stop and search black travelers on any pretense, again using drug searches as an excuse.

Inez, a twenty-one-year-old dark-skinned woman from New York, recounted her experience at a Virginia airport:

> Returning from an overnight trip to New York, I arrived at Langston International Airport in Virginia with only an overnight bag. I went outside the airport to look for my ride to Norfolk State University. While walking down a pathway to the parking lot, something told me to turn around. I did. I saw two white men. Jokingly, I said to myself, "They're probably following me."
>
> Much to my dismay, soon after I turned around, they manhandled me, took me in the bushes, and searched my bag. I asked them, "What are you looking for?" They said, "Drugs." I was shocked. I couldn't believe they would suspect me. They asked, "Where did you get the school books in your bag? How long did you stay in New York? Did you have business there? Why are you in Virginia?" Subsequently, they requested my identification.
>
> When they didn't find drugs and determined my identity, they told me to close my bags and left without an apology. Afterward, I spoke with a man, the black gardener who worked there, who had watched the search. He told me that only blacks were searched. I felt angry; I wanted to confront the police officers, but I was afraid. I thought to myself, "You never know what they will do to a black girl. Keep your mouth shut."

Most of the young college men at Norfolk State University with whom I spoke had stories to tell about being stopped and searched. Armed with police equipment, many white police officers not only stop and search young black men, but they use threats, sometimes very frightening ones, for greater effect. Antwan, twenty-one and living in Pennsylvania, told this story. On one occasion, a police officer approached Antwan and signaled for him to pull off the road. With a .357 Magnum aimed at Antwan's face, the police officer said, "This is my baby [gun]. If you try something funny, you're going to get my baby." Police equipment was often reportedly used to instill the fear of death in innocent young black men. This type of threat usually worked. "The first thing that came to my mind," Antwan said, "was this officer is going to kill me. To prevent death, I tried to be as calm as possible."

Since Antwan was in his own neighborhood when this happened and his neighbors had witnessed the incident, a few of them went to Antwan's home and brought his parents to the scene. After the officer drew his gun, he told Antwan to open the car door slowly. Antwan reported:

> I did exactly what he said, so that he wouldn't have an excuse to shoot me. The officer continued telling me to slowly reach under the seat to retrieve my license. I handed my license to him and told him that I was driving my mother's car, and that she kept the registration card in her wallet. Then the officer put away his gun and proceeded to write tickets worth $200.

At about that time, Antwan's parents arrived. Since no violations had occurred to warrant the tickets, the police officer said little to Antwan's parents, who took the officer's badge number and name. When they got home, they called the police station and talked with a high-ranking official, who promised a visit from a police representative to explain the situation and apologize. No representative ever came to their home.

Feeling that his rights had been violated, Antwan took his tickets to traffic court and gave this account of his experience:

> The white judge asked the officer to tell his side of the story. The officer told the judge that I was speeding on a residential street, driving recklessly, endangering people's lives, and driving without a registration card. I didn't have the registration card at the time, but everything else was untrue.

The judge asked me to tell my side of the story. I told the judge exactly what had happened. The judge's expression changed from warm to angry. The judge, everyone in the courtroom, and I knew what the judge really wanted to say, but he told the officer, "You did your job." The judge, however, found me not guilty, and I wasn't fined.

Unlike Antwan, most college students chose not to seek relief from judges, assuming that these judges would be no more understanding than the police officers had been. Judges, on all levels of our court system, should not unquestioningly accept incorrect police reports. They need to clamp down on police officers and require them to present true information about arrests. When police officers submit a limited number of erroneous reports on arrested persons, they should be dismissed. In all cases police officers and judges should dismiss blacks whose accusation is not substantiated by well-grounded facts.

Alongside making threats, many white officers attempted to demean and harass the young black men they stopped as much as possible. The police officers variously required the young men to lay face down on the road, called for backup, used racial slurs, and were otherwise verbally abusive. Truitt, twenty-five and from New Jersey, told this story:

It was February 1993, and I was twenty-three years old. I was traveling by car from New Jersey to North Carolina. About thirty minutes into the trip, a white police officer pulled me over and said that I was driving ninety miles an hour; however, I had only been doing sixty. The officer rudely made me get out of my car and ordered me to lie face down on the side of the highway. He called for backup and then began searching my car for drugs. While I was lying on the ground, the officer shouted out to me, "Nigger. I know you got drugs. Where are they?" I said, "There are no drugs." Then he answered back by saying, "Your black ass is going to jail today." Not finding drugs, he only wrote a speeding ticket and let me go. After driving away, I felt rage because it seems as if blacks can't get true justice in America.

These demeaning techniques are taken even further. Often white police officers ordered the students to put their arms on the car and to straddle their legs. This is often followed by irrelevant and humiliating questions. Victor, twenty-one, had this experience:

My friend's parents gave him a new car as his high school graduation gift. He was nineteen years old. One day he came over to my house to show me his new car then take me for a ride. We were in Chesapeake, Virginia. A police officer stopped us and made us get out of the car and straddle our legs with our hands and arms spread on the side of the car. Then the police officer asked my friend what kind of work he did. My friend said, "I work at a restaurant." The cop said, "You don't make enough money to afford this kind of car." My friend said, "It was a graduation gift." The cop never told us why he stopped us in the first place, but he told us we could leave.

The students reported another angle to these unwarranted stops and searches. Often white police officers feel compelled to turn them into dramatic productions. This frequent occurrence was described by Jobe, a twenty-year-old student:

In the summer of 1992, when I was nineteen years old, I spent a couple of weeks in New Haven, Connecticut, with my family. This is basically an urban area with more blacks than whites. One day we decided to drive to Hamden, which is more suburban. This area is white with a few blacks. While driving, I noticed a cop sounding the siren on his car and signaling me to pull over. I pulled over and turned off my car. He told us to put our hands up slowly and slowly extend them out the car window. He finally came over to the car. Before I could even ask what had happened, additional police officers arrived and handcuffed us. They made us sit on the ground with our legs crossed while they searched the car. My cousin, the driver, told them where the registration, insurance papers, and license were located. Then they let us go and told us that it had been a misunderstanding. They said that a car with the same model, year, and color had been reported stolen. My cousin and I felt that because we were four black men, ages nineteen to twenty-one, we were stopped because of our race and youth. When they were searching the car, they were most likely looking for drugs and guns. We felt humiliated by being forced to sit on the ground in handcuffs with high beams shining in our faces. After everything was cleaned up, the officers didn't even attempt to apologize. All they said was, "Oh well, mistakes happen."

Bill, twenty-one, reported a similar experience:

I was in the Bronx, New York, on my way to visit friends from school. I had two of my friends in the jeep with me. I had a stereo system; therefore, the music was loud. We were getting off the George Washington Bridge, and we made a right turn. In that block, there was a police car approaching, so I lowered the music and proceeded normally. At the next corner, police officers pulled in front of our car with their lights flashing and guns drawn. They ordered us out of the jeep with our hands in the air. When we got out of the jeep, one officer hand-cuffed and searched me. He stepped back, and his partner did the same to my friends. One cop said, after I asked what was going on, "We had reason to believe that you may have been transporting drugs across state lines." He asked for my license and registration card. Of course, the registration card was in my friend's name. Consequently, he ran checks on me, and his police partner proceeded to search the vehicle. I watched him closely to make sure that he didn't place anything in the jeep. He didn't find anything that was illegal. Then they let us go. My reaction was anger, as was my friend's. We knew that, without reason, except that we were black and driving a luxury automobile, we were treated like criminals. I felt resentment, but I decided that it wasn't the first time and that it probably wouldn't be the last time. After all, I am a young black male. It was a nice summer day. I was young, carefree, expecting to have fun. Instead, I became scared to death knowing that if I made one false move I could be killed. It was a scary experience. I had trusted white people, but since that incident, I haven't trusted them.

Will, twenty-three, described the drama cooked up by the police officers who had stopped him for no reason:

The worst racist experience that I have had with a white person was when I was driving down Virginia Beach Boulevard and was pulled over by two white policemen. They asked me to step out of my car. According to them I fit a criminal profile. They began searching my car. They asked me how could I afford an Acura Legend since I was only twenty years old. I told them that it was none of their business and asked if I could leave. They replied, "No. Shut up." Then they proceeded to search my car. When they didn't find anything, they let me go and said they would be watching me. I asked, "For what?" They said, "You better watch yourself."

The story always seems to be the same. Being black and owning nice cars are many police officers' guidelines for stopping young blacks, though they will usually use drugs or speeding as their excuses. In the process, high drama often dominates.

WHEN IT'S NOT EVEN SAFE TO TAKE A WALK

Many police officers also stopped and searched young blacks traveling on foot. These encounters are similar to those behind the wheel. Irwin, twenty-one and living in Virginia, related this encounter:

My friend Lester and I were walking home from work one night. It was late when we got off. It just so happened that we walked by a restaurant that had just been robbed. Several policemen stopped and pointed their guns and night sticks at us. They made us lay on the ground, and one of them stuck something painful and sharp in my back. Next, they started reading me the Miranda: "You have the right to remain silent," etc. I never knew what the sharp object in my back was until my friend told me that it was a gun. I thought that it was a night stick. While we asked questions about our treatment, the police officer continued to tell us to shut up before they gave us something to complain about. They implied that they were going to beat us. They never asked us any questions. They arrested us because we were black.

The police officers believed that because the restaurant was robbed, the robbers must have been black. Since we were in the neighborhood, we were guilty. I just couldn't believe that. I couldn't believe that because the robbers were assumed to be black, we were made out to be the robbers. During this time, a man ran across the railroad tracks. Some of the police officers ran to catch him. When they caught him, he had several hundred dollar bills. They were still holding us on the ground in handcuffs. The man had a dark mask in his jacket pocket. When they turned him around in the light, one police officer said, "Oh my goodness. He's white." The policemen were totally astounded. Before they let us go, they asked the man if we were his accomplices. He said, "No." The police officers never apologized to us. All this time, the gun was still sticking in my back. Finally, they took the handcuffs off us, and we went home. By the way, the setting was a well-known location in Williamsburg, Virginia. This is the worst experience that I've ever had with white people.

How sad that two young blacks can't even walk down the street in a nice neighborhood without encountering false arrest, threats, racist stereotypes, and implied violence. White police officers should realize that whites commit the same crimes as blacks.

Ellis, twenty-three, related a variation of this experience, which occurred in his small hometown in North Carolina. On the predominantly black side of town, the police always searched black males riding in cars at the park. They also sat outside housing complexes watching the actions of all the blacks moving around in the community. He said, "It makes me feel like blacks are prisoners rather than slaves." In that town, black youngsters often went to the gym to play basketball. Police officers randomly stopped, frisked, and searched the children when they entered and left the gyms. Ellis concluded by saying, "This makes me feel like I don't belong in my own hometown." White police officers erroneously stop and search blacks of all ages: Even children aren't free to go to the gym for healthy fun without police interference. These white police officers introduced young children to racism among police officers. This is the kind of policing that could make black children believe they ought to misbehave: If it's expected of them anyway, maybe that's what they're supposed to be doing. Children only need to see and hear something once to remember it for a lifetime.

Jerome, thirty-two and an Illinois resident, described another variation of being stopped as a pedestrian:

One of my worst experiences with racism occurred when I was visiting my brother, who lived in one of the wealthiest areas of Chicago, Hyde Park. It was 1991, and I was home from the military for the visit. At the time, I was twenty-three years old and was visiting my brother for the first time in his new house. One day while I was walking down a street, I noticed a police car following me. When I turned around to see what the police officer wanted, he suddenly drove up beside me, rolled his window down, and asked, "What are you doing over here?" I told him that America is a free country, and that I could go anywhere I desired. I know this was a stupid thing to say, but this happened around the time of the Los Angeles riots and the Rodney King controversy, so I felt militant and defiant. The officer turned off the car, got out, pushed me against the car, and told me to "spread 'em." I spread my legs, and he frisked me like I had just robbed the First National Bank of Chicago. This included pulling my shirt out of my pants, turning my pockets inside out, and running his fingers through my hair. I felt humiliated. He then asked me again in a loud voice, "Where are you going?" In an angry loud voice, I yelled, "Over to my brother's house." He said, "You must think I'm a fool. Everybody knows niggers are too poor to live over here." Then, he said, "You can't buy a house with food stamps." Then I remembered the Rodney King thing and said to myself, "Oh, no, not another Rodney King experience." I was relieved, however, when he said that he would escort me to my brother's house. To this day, I thank God that my brother was at home. If he hadn't been there, I probably would have been required to spend the night in jail. Before that experience, I wasn't really sure of what I wanted to do with the degree I am earning in criminal justice. Now I am clear about what I want to do. I plan to join the police force, work my way up, and make a difference in the way police officers practice law enforcement in this country. I don't want to do this from the outside carrying a picket sign; I want to do it from the inside, behind a desk, whose sign reads POLICE CHIEF.

Far from the Windy City, Ralph, twenty-four, was subjected to another variation of the search process when he was a young college student:

> I was in the Orange Projects in Orange, New Jersey. It was the summer of 1993, and I was twenty-two years old. I was sitting in my car talking with my friend, who lives in the projects. We were just hanging out. A police car came through the block once. Later, they made a second trip down the block, stopped, and ordered us away from the car. One officer searched both of us, and the other officer searched my car. I was getting angrier by the minute. Everyone whom we knew in the projects was watching. It was embarrassing. We had not committed a crime. I asked one officer what the problem was. He replied, "Just stand there and shut up." The other officer said, "Someone reported gunshots being fired in the courtyard by two black men fitting your description." After finding nothing on either of us and nothing in my car, we were released and told to have a good night. I felt outraged. It was such an abuse of authority. I felt hatred. I wanted to fight them and hurt them physically because my pride had been hurt, and I was embarrassed. I went home to my girlfriend and basked in the comfort of her love. I told her what had happened. She was just as angry. I lay awake all night thinking only about what I could do. Actually, there was nothing that I could do, except not be defeated. That is, I decided not to change the person that I was because of other people's ignorance.

Ralph's story is the story of millions of blacks locked in housing projects all over the nation. It indicates the enormous amount of abusive police power against poor blacks living in housing developments. This case clarifies the conditions of poor blacks enough for police chiefs around the country to want to train their officers to allow innocent poor blacks to enjoy what little they have. Ralph's story goes beyond that. It indicates that innocent blacks cannot walk, ride, or sit without being harassed by the police. Federal, state, and city legislators should reform the corrupt police departments in this land. Let every American stand up now for the eradication of this kind of police corruption—subjection of innocent blacks to criminal procedures.

HARASSMENT AND UNEQUAL TREATMENT

The young students also reported various cases of being dangerously harassed by white police officers. Elizabeth, twenty-one, stated:

> Some time last fall in Piscataway, New Jersey, when my friend and I were returning from a festival in New York City, something terrifying happened. Looking through my rearview mirror, I noticed a police car following us. I kept driving the fifty-five-miles-per-hour speed limit. Suddenly, a police officer swerved his car and tried to hit our car. To avoid a deliberate accident, I swerved our car in the opposite direction. The police officer tried twice again to hit our car. Unable to win at swerving, the officer stopped harassing us and drove away. I was upset, scared, and angry.

White policemen often seem to make up and enforce their own laws.[1] Countless experiences support this point. For example, Fletcher, twenty-four and from New York, related:

> On January 4, 1993, I was returning to Norfolk State University when I was pulled over to the side of the highway in Salisbury, Maryland. Even though I appeared to be driving the only vehicle on the road that particular morning, I drove within the speed limit. It was a clear, cold, wintry morning. The sun had just begun to rise. I had the sun roof in my car partially open while listening to jazz. It was a comfortable ride.

Soon, however, a red 5.0 Mustang joined me on the highway. The Mustang got behind me, followed, and tailgated with its high beams on. I started to panic but kept my composure. I recollect putting on my right signal light and changing lanes. The Mustang pulled up beside me. The driver rolled down his passenger window, did the dozens (stuck his thumb up in the air) and smiled while he drove faster. I remember my heart beating fast and hard. It felt as if it were in my mouth. I couldn't help but notice his long blonde hair and crystal blue eyes.

Approximately three to four miles ahead, there was a brown Caprice Classic Chevrolet parked on the shoulder of the highway, facing oncoming traffic. As I approached the car, the white man in the car looked at me the same time that I looked in his direction. However, I didn't want to take any chances because I didn't know whether he was a state trooper. I set my cruise control at fifty-five miles per hour and coasted down the highway while I periodically glanced in my rearview mirror. By the way he looked, I felt that he was going to turn around and follow me. Slowly but surely, he crept up on my left side in the passing lane. I continued to drive the normal speed, and he continued to look over at me, and we rode side by side until he dropped behind me and stuck his hand out the window, flagging me to pull over. Nevertheless, I continued driving. Then he reached over to the passenger seat, got his hat, put it on, and turned on his flashing blue lights mounted in the grill of his vehicle.

When I pulled over, the police officer walked up to my car with his hand on his gun. He said, "Sir, step out of the vehicle." I did. He went on to ask, "Why didn't you pull over earlier when I flagged you?" I replied, "I am sorry, officer, but I didn't know who you were in the unmarked car, and you never turned on your lights." The police officer said, "License, registration, and insurance card." He then said, "Sir, come back to my car with me." We sat in the policeman's car while he radioed for backup. Four police cars arrived within two minutes.

He then asked, "Sir, do you know where you are?" I replied, "Yes, Maryland." He said, "This is a small town by the name of Salisbury." His next question was "What's your destination this early in the morning?" I said, "Norfolk State University, where I attend college." He then said, "Step out of the car while the other officers ask you questions." They asked me such questions as, "Whose car is this?" and "Who's Samuel and Lydia Johnson?" I told them that it was my car, that my parents had co-signed for the car, and that was the reason their names were on my registration card.

Then one of the officers told me to place my hands on top of my head while he searched me. Officer number two asked, "Are you in a rush?" I said, "Yes." He replied, "This won't take long." He somewhat forced me to sign forms that gave them permission to search my car. I was aware that once I signed my name on the forms, my rights had been waived. Two officers stayed at my side questioning me while the other two literally tore my car apart. They disconnected the speakers, took my suitcases out, looked under the hood, disconnected the battery, and more.

At this time, I could feel tears rolling down my face. I asked, "Officer, can you tell me why you stopped me?" He answered, "I got on my radar that someone was speeding, and I didn't know if it was the 5.0 Mustang or you." I asked, "What are you looking for?" One officer said, "We get a lot of drugs coming through our state, and we want to put a stop to it." After about one and a half hours, they decided to let me go, but it took me twenty-five minutes to put everything back in place in my car. No ticket, no apology, and no courtesy was extended.

Johnny Van, twenty-three and from Connecticut, had a similar experience. He was on his way back to Norfolk State University and was about ninety minutes from his destination. He was following a white man, who was driving about eighty miles an hour. Johnny Van was driving about seventy-five miles per hour. After a while he slowed down, because, as he put it, he was "asking for it."

I got it as we approached Eastville, Virginia. A trooper was parked outside a diner on my right-hand side. This was about 7:30 in the morning. The trooper let the white man, who was driving ten to fifteen miles faster than I was driving, continue, but he pulled me over. When I spotted the officer, I began slowing down. When I saw that he didn't have a radar gun, I was not too worried, but I was wrong not to be. He let the white man in the Oldsmobile Cutlass and business suit go and pulled over the young black male, who was twenty-one years of age, because he might be a criminal.

But here's the catch. The way he pulled me over was that he claimed he had traveled seventy miles an hour to get on my tail; this technique is called PACE. That's how he had determined how fast I was going. After he pulled me over, I was upset and frustrated because I couldn't do a thing about it. He took my license and registration card to his car and stayed there about half an hour.

When he came back to my car, he tried to hold a conversation with me. The first thing that came out of my mouth was, "Did you see the white guy in front of me speeding?" He said, "No." I knew this was total bull, so I took the ticket from him. He asked, "Where are you going to school?" I said, "School." Then he started looking through my back window to see if I was carrying drugs or something. I started my car and didn't give him a chance to say anything else. I pulled off, and he followed me for about ten miles and then turned around. As of now, I am waiting to go to court to tell the judge my side of the story.

Young college students reported other incidents of white people receiving better treatment from police officers. For example, often when whites were at fault in car accidents involving blacks, the police officers would release them from any responsibility. Jerome, for example, reported that a white man had hit his car one night. He was drunk, obviously at fault, and had no insurance. A white police officer was called to the scene of the accident. After looking at the damage, the police officer told Jerome to leave. Jerome was upset. He said, "The police officer represented the law and was not doing his job correctly. I felt as if the system had failed me. I resolved to sue the man; the case is now being tried."

What becomes most clear from these stories is that white police officers in America often don't follow the written law in their dealings with black people. Rather, they devise their own rules, rules that allow them to needlessly stop, search, threaten, and harass young blacks. And what many young black people find so painful is that their experiences with the law are so drastically different from what most white people experience.

SECURITY OFFICERS AND BOUNCERS

Many young college men reported being harassed as much by security officers as they were by the police. The only difference was the techniques used. Morton, for example, told me that he was looking for a hair-styling product in a particular store. A white salesman followed him around the store. Soon he asked Morton, who was twenty when we spoke and living in Virginia, to accompany him to the manager's office. When they got there, the security officer looked in Morton's bag to see if he had stolen something, but nothing was found.

Another young college man described this encounter with a security officer:

When I was twelve years old or a little younger, I was in a drugstore. I was looking for a G.I. Joe doll, but I didn't have any money. It was my intent to browse and see how cool the figure was and decide whether I wanted to buy it later. Soon a store attendant, a tall white guy, asked me what I was doing in the store. I asked to see G.I. Joe. Irritated, he led me to the area. I checked the doll out, said "Thanks," and put it back. He said, "Look, you don't want anything here. So just leave." I was shocked by his reaction. I was a potential customer. I'm sure he suspected me of stealing. I was confused because this was new to me. I went home, but I didn't say anything to Mama because I didn't know how to handle it.

Not only did the security officers in stores harass young college men, but, in at least one case, university security officers harassed a college student. Foster, twenty-two and from Virginia, said:

Last year I attended Freak Nic in Atlanta, Georgia. Freak Nic is a festival that attracts a large number of black students every year. I was driving near Larsen University. Irene was hanging out of the sun roof of my car. A Larsen University security officer pulled me over and started questioning me. He asked me who the car belonged to, where we were going, what we were doing in Atlanta, and other irrelevant questions. Then he asked me whether I had been drinking. I said that I had drunk a little whiskey, and he gave me a sobriety test. When the meter read that I wasn't drunk, he called a female security officer. She came and asked me the same stupid questions. Then she looked at the meter and asked the male security officer if he wanted to take me in. I thought to myself, "What a bitch."

Luckily, a white student at Larsen University rode by and yelled out his window, "Since you're not on our campus, they can't pull you over. I am a Larsen University student; I know. They're just doing that to you because you're black and not from around here." And I'll be damned if the officer didn't tell me to get back into my car and carry on.

Many students noted that police and security officers alike consistently asked them the same kinds of pointless questions. I can confidently report that apart from everything else, young black students are tired of being asked the same things again and again for no reason. A graver similarity between stories about the police and stories about security officers is that their actions were consistently unwarranted and based on racist beliefs rather than on necessity.

Many young male students reported going to white night clubs, sometimes having encounters with bouncers, whom they regarded as a kind of police. Roosevelt, a twenty-four-year-old Virginia resident, related this encounter, which did end up involving the police:

> In June 1993, some friends and I went to Virginia Beach on a Saturday afternoon. We decided to go to a bar and get some drinks. Since there aren't any black-owned bars on the oceanfront, we settled for what was there. We went to the door of one bar, and immediately a bouncer approached my friend and asked for his identification. My friend showed him an I.D. The bouncer said that we couldn't get in without a membership card.
>
> My friend didn't believe him, so he asked another employee, who said that we needed a membership card or a Virginia driver's license to get in. The bouncer grabbed my friend, but my friend ducked away. Then the bouncer grabbed my friend by the head, and the other bouncers at the club ran to the door. Consequently, my friends and I ran to the door, where people were pushing and shoving. Then they closed the door.
>
> As soon as we turned around, we saw that some police officers were there. They had to have seen what had happened. The bouncers came outside yelling for the police to arrest us. The police said, "When something like this happens, the police are required to get one group's information and switch it with the other group's report." Well, he got our information but forgot to obtain theirs. My friend is verbal and militant. He started pointing out the people whose

information he wanted. The police got the information. Then we left the club.

About two weeks later, we received warrants in the mail. We're supposed to go to court in September. We are mad as hell. The warrants are senseless. None of us used any violence or did anything wrong.

We don't have space here to follow these black middle-class youths through the court system. Suffice it to say that although some were made to pay fines, none of them was arrested legally, and none of them was declared guilty of a crime or imprisoned.

WHAT TO DO ABOUT IT

Racism, a dreaded organism in any system, is even more virulent when it shows up in law enforcement systems. Police officers often have a major impact on the lives of young blacks, especially young men. Police officers are armed with official power and deadly force. How they read situations, such as traffic compliance, affects which persons are stopped and whether these persons are subject to physical injury and even threat of death.

What White People Can Do

Countering racism in the police system must begin at the top. The police chief and commissioners set the tone in every police department and unit. A police chief who practices racism will encourage others to do likewise. In such an environment, white police officers will feel free (perhaps even encouraged) to treat blacks unjustly. Innocent young black people may be threatened, verbally abused, falsely accused or arrested, manhandled, beaten, and sometimes even killed.

A well-intentioned police chief, in contrast, sets a standard of equality and fairness and insists that everyone in the department lives up to this standard. He or she implements strict policies for ensuring equality and justice, enforcing these policies when officers fail to comply with them.

White police officers have many opportunities to treat young black men unfairly, but there are just as many opportunities for fair-minded, well-intentioned police officers to behave justly. Police officers who truly believe in justice will not prejudge young black men and will treat them with impartiality and respect. This includes not acting on the presumption that any young black man in a large or expensive car is either a drug dealer or a car thief. To be sure, young black men deal in drugs and steal cars—as do young men of other races—but it is unjust to stop motorists just because of the model of their car. Many young blacks drive cars loaned or given to them by their parents; others have worked hard at legitimate jobs in order to purchase such automobiles. These blacks, like anyone else, deserve to drive down the street free from hassle and harassment.

How white police officers choose to talk to black people is another vital issue. Many never resort to verbal abuse because they don't have to. These officers are smart enough to find better, more effective ways of communicating with people. Besides, these officers respect themselves too much to lower themselves to this type of bad behavior. Good officers know that calling people names doesn't work anyway. Calling a black man "boy" or using ugly racial slurs such as "nigger" doesn't command respect or inspire cooperation. Usually it provokes resistance and defiance, creating even more fear and mistrust.

On many occasions white police officers in the legitimate execution of their duties need to approach black people. Some black people, of course, do break the law, just as some white people do. And there are times, during investigations, when police officers need to interact with blacks who have not committed a crime but who may be behaving suspiciously. The key here is to treat everyone with the same dignity and respect. If an officer pulls over a black motorist for speeding, for instance, then no special show of force is needed. In more serious situations, additional reinforcement may be necessary, but no more than is used when the suspect is white. And if a white driver is found speeding on the same road, then he or she should be pulled over as well.

Many white police officers follow such sensible guidelines: They behave fairly and equally by nature. Unfortunately, too many police officers do not. Therefore, police departments need to implement training and development programs specifically targeted to eliminating racist behaviors. Police departments can incorporate communication skills into their training programs, along with courses on self-control and relationship skills. And such training needs to be repeated periodically, perhaps involving members of the black community.

Equally important, police officers should be trained to distinguish between guilty and nonguilty persons. A policy should be implemented in each department to prevent police officers from stopping blacks randomly. When police officers decide to interfere with blacks who are driving, walking, and sitting, they should have specific legal grounds for doing so. Most important of all, white racist police officers should not be permitted on police forces. Among the whites, only men and women who respect blacks and possess personal integrity and dignity should be hired. Policing integrity and dignity are what count—not a well-decorated uniform.

To straighten out police departments in America—and almost all need help—action has to be taken to put police chiefs in office who will develop staffs that become famous and beloved because of their high morality, integrity, decency, and dignity. That kind of character circumvents racism. This can be accomplished. We need to make sure that weaklings, racists, and overly domineering people never get the top jobs. Our police departments need heads who know how to run clean, honest, fair, and efficient departments. We have talked long enough. Legal justice for black America is overdue. White America, stand up and clean up every police department in this country. Blacks can't do it. They are the victims. White people can. Please accept the challenge.

Everything I have said about the police system applies equally to the entire legal system. Judges, prosecutors, and other court officials also need to be fair-minded if racism is ever to be eliminated. Many judges listen open-mindedly to both sides of every case, even when a white police officer and a young black male are involved. Judicial decisions at all levels should be based solely on the evidence and in no way influenced by personal attitudes, prejudices, criminal profiles, or assumptions. Every white person needs to insist that these standards are followed in their communities, from police chief to police officers, from judges to prosecutors. Nothing enhances a community's moral climate more than to have the public law enforcement system under a watchful public eye.

I recommend that both police chiefs and district attorneys run for election for three-year terms. Voters should listen to campaign speeches and choose the fairest, less racist candidates. And they should vote them out if they don't get rid of injustice to blacks. All Americans are asked to start at the beginning of this century to use the ballot to reform the police departments in this nation. This country needs to provide the black population with the confidence that the high morality in the police departments and district attorneys' offices will allow them to live like other people. Any city, including New York and Los Angeles, can take the lead in molding finer police officers. Black justice in the legal system should be the goal of every city, county, and state. There is no time left for dragging our feet.

What Black People Can Do

Black people, particularly young black men, also have a role to play in improving relations between the black community and law enforcement agencies. Driving responsibly not only contributes to a safer community, but it also enhances the freedom and pleasure of being behind the wheel or out on the streets. People of any color should not give up celebrating their individuality or cultural heritage, but they should make wise choices. Appearance can go a long way toward signaling a person's good intentions. Clothing or behavior that suggests to police officers belonging to a street gang or drug ring is going to draw their immediate attention.

Decent behavior works both ways. When police officers stop young black people, these young people should walk with their bodies erect, look officers in the eye, and speak respectfully. The officers should do the same. Polite replies, even to insulting questions, can help diffuse a threatening situation. The more that blacks do to demonstrate that they are decent members of society, the more willing police officers—starting with the ones who already behave fairly—will be to admit they've made a mistake when they have.

Blacks can also be proactive when it comes to dealings with police officers. When stopped unfairly or treated badly, get the officer's name and number. Then report the incident to the officer's superiors. Black community leaders can also be informed. When enough of these kinds of reports accumulate, the system has to give. It's time for black people to work on not inviting unwanted trouble. And it's also time for all blacks to object in public forums, through community-action coalitions, and in local political circles to uncover and root out racism.

6

FROM EATING OUT
TO WORKING OUT

We have seen that young middle-class college students experience racism in their neighborhoods, at school, while shopping, on the job, and with law enforcement officials. The stories about these experiences were prompted by my question, What were your three most racist experiences? Another question, Where are the most difficult places to go? also prompted a wealth of responses. The stories that the students told in response to this question, about recreational settings, walking and other means of transportation, and farms, make up this last chapter. These stories concern the everyday life of blacks and go a long way toward illuminating the kind of racism that most black people face daily.

RECREATIONAL SETTINGS

The students I spoke with saw people all around them enjoying themselves. They wanted to be able to enjoy themselves in the same ways. They described racist encounters in various recreational settings that ended up depriving them of the pleasure they sought. Often they described their pleasure turning quickly to anger and hurt.

Middle-class Americans, including blacks, eat out on average more than 3.5 times a week. Black people, just like whites, want to enjoy eating out. Often, because of unpleasant encounters, they will not. Often blacks know they don't get their money's worth at restaurants. Young blacks know it too. The students had some of their most difficult experiences with racism in restaurants. Reports of simply not being waited on were common. Michelle, twenty-two and from South Carolina, said:

> I went to a restaurant in Virginia with three of my friends. We waited a long time to be served. After several couples had entered the restaurant after us and been served, we still had not been helped. We asked if there was a problem. The wait-ress said, "Yes, there is. You're not supposed to be here." We asked, "How can that be the case in the 1980s?" She said, "Let me get my manager." He came to our table and said, "We're crowded. If you don't leave, I'll call the police." Because we were not rude or loud, there was no reason for them not to serve us; therefore, we told him to call the police.
>
> When the officers arrived, they told him that he was required to serve us. He said, "I would rather close the place down than serve blacks." After arguing with the police, he finally said that he would serve us. When he asked what we wanted, we told him, "No, thank you." We felt that if he didn't want to serve us, he was in the wrong; consequently, we didn't want to give him our money. It was the principle behind it. We simply went elsewhere. Until this day, I've never returned to that restaurant.

Many young blacks reported experiencing a classic racist prac-tice in restaurants: being told "Our tables are all reserved." Gregory, who was twenty years old when we spoke and from Virginia, described what happened to him in a restaurant when he was eigh-teen years old. He and some friends were returning home from a party at around two A.M. They were hungry and drove around for thirty minutes looking for somewhere to eat. They finally found a place that was open. There were about thirty white people inside. When Gregory looked through the window, he saw four unused tables. They walked inside, and everyone in the restaurant turned around and stared at them as if they, in Gregory's words, were Martians. When they approached the hostess and asked her to seat them, she looked at them as though they were crazy and said, "We have no more seats available."

Gregory's friend asked, "What do you mean there are no more seats available?" The waitress replied, "Those tables are reserved." Gregory asked, "Has someone reserved four tables to eat breakfast at three o'clock in the morning?" She answered, "Yes." Gregory said, "This is foolishness. Since we're here, you can serve us, because we only need one table." She said, "No. We can't do that." One of the young men became loud and asked, "Is it because we're black?" She said, "No." They told the waitress that there are too many restaurants in this world to have to put up with that "bull." They left, slamming the door. Racism keeps blacks on the run everywhere—including at restaurants.

The students also reported that they commonly waited longer than white customers to be seated. In many black people's eyes, there is little difference between no service and slow service. Most blacks are understandably sensitive about who arrives first, how reservations are honored, and in what order people are seated and served. Kelly, twenty-two and from Minnesota, stated, "My friends and I had made reservations at a restaurant. When we arrived, the white maître d' overlooked our reservations and kept us waiting twenty minutes to be seated."

When blacks are not seated in a timely manner, it's because whites arriving later are seated first, or because white hosts and hostesses say there are only seats available in the smoking section or there is a twenty- to thirty-minute waiting period. Blacks know there are empty tables in the nonsmoking section. They know it doesn't take twenty-five minutes to clean a table. So what they intended to be fine dining becomes anger and unpleasantness. The hosts and hostesses know that's enough to either ruin their meal or send them away.

Although Lillian was seated on time in a Virginia restaurant, the service was off schedule:

> In 1992, I went to a restaurant at five P.M. for dinner with some other people. We were seated in the proper order. However, we noticed that white diners, seated after us, were served first. After this pattern had continued for thirty minutes, we confronted the waitresses. They told us there was no waitress in our section, but we couldn't take that excuse. Consequently, we left and never returned.

Jennifer, nineteen and a resident of Delaware, reported a similar experience:

> One Saturday night my friends and I went to a national-chain restaurant for dinner. We entered the diner and were immediately seated. Until we had sat there and complained for twenty to twenty-five minutes, a server never set the table, never gave us water or even a menu. After a big deal, we were finally given a menu. When we were ready to place our orders, no one was around. We waited another twenty to twenty-five minutes and again began complaining. The servers passed our table and said, "I am not your waitress" or "She'll soon be with you."
>
> If the restaurant had been crowded, I could have understood. Each time I glimpsed our waitress, she was idle and talking with waitresses in the back of the diner. After an hour, we still had not placed our orders. Finally, the waitress came to our table, and there was a big altercation. We told her that we didn't want to eat there, that we would never come back, that the service stank, that she would hear from us. Then we left.

Shelton, twenty-one and from North Carolina, related a similar occurrence at another restaurant:

> In the beginning of July 1993, six of my buddies and I tried to get breakfast at two A.M. After club hopping, we walked into a restaurant to get a meal. We sat down, and a white woman who looked to be in her mid-thirties said, "Oh, goodness. I'll be back." That was the first and last time that we saw her. We heard her in the kitchen screaming, "I ain't serving them. Somebody better help table four." Ten minutes later, after a great deal of discussion, a black waitress came out and apologized for the mess and asked if she could take our order. We had decided that we were no longer hungry and left.

Managers and servers should either require all customers to pay before being served or they should stop this practice with blacks. I have only been asked to pay before being served once, but it was so humiliating that I count it as one of the worst racist experiences I had ever had. Americans know they don't pay for a sit-down meal before eating. Yet the college men and women reported having been required to do just that. Candice, a twenty-year-old resident of Maryland, related her experience:

> We entered a restaurant and ordered our meal. As soon as we had been served, unlike other customers, we were asked to pay immediately. I don't know why our waitress treated us that way. I left angry and disturbed. Of course, I'll never again go to that restaurant.

Racial slurs are also often part of a black person's dining experience. Claudine, nineteen and from Virginia, gave this example:

> I experienced racism in a restaurant in Virginia. One Sunday my friends and I decided to meet at a restaurant. When we

entered the dining room, there were tables available in the back near the door and up front near the television. We proceeded to one of the front tables and passed five to eight white men, who appeared to be between thirty-nine and sixty years of age, who were watching football on the television. Their mean stares made us uncomfortable. At the same time, they hurled a few racial slurs. After we sat at the front table, all the men left, and we had control of everything. This is a case where racism gave blacks space and an opportunity to have fun.

The students also had difficulty in restaurants when they requested separate checks. Although the students' differing financial circumstances often warranted receiving separate checks, this request was often met with racist responses. Melody, twenty-one and from New York, related one of those experiences:

Six friends and I went out one Saturday night. We entered the restaurant and were seated at a table by the white waiter, who looked to be in his mid twenties. After everyone had decided what to order, the waiter returned. Before ordering, we asked him to make out separate checks. He told us that he couldn't do that and that we had to pay as one person. We told him that some of us planned to pay cash while others would use charge cards. In a nasty tone, the waiter stated, "Whoever is paying cash is required to give their money to those using credit cards." All of us knew that was ridiculous. We told the rude server that we had eaten in that restaurant three times and never had a problem paying separately. I asked how he could assume that everybody knew each other well enough to put the total bill on one credit card. He replied, "Well, you have a problem. You either have to do it my way or leave." We knew we were not going anywhere until we were served. We asked, "May we split up by payment plan and sit at separate tables?" He responded, "No. You can't come in as two separate parties." Then he proceeded to take our orders while acting rude by talking over some of us and acknowledging only the people with whom he desired to speak. We demanded to see the manager. After the waiter refused to get the manager, we finally flagged down another waiter and demanded that he get the manager. He did. The manager finally served us himself and apologized for the waiter's ill behavior. He also said that he would deal with him. Then he rang up different totals as we had requested.

And sometimes the young people told of experiencing several different types of racist behavior during one meal. Jeffrey told this story:

After a big football game one Friday night, a friend and I stopped at a restaurant connected to a national chain. It was packed. So we were seated for about ten minutes waiting to be called for a table. They ran out of hamburger meat and obtained a box from another store. Finally, the white waiter told us in a nasty voice to be seated at a table. And then he told us it would take ten minutes to prepare our food. We said fine. It took much longer. When our food was ready, our waiter refused to serve us. He tried to get another waiter to serve us, but that waiter refused. The manager told the first waiter to serve us. He refused and said, "Forget them niggas. Let them come and get it." The manager asked him, "How would you feel if a nigga had your job?" He replied, "Ain't no nigga gonna get this job." The manager said, "We'll see." She asked, "How about one of you boys working here?" We didn't take the job, but she didn't charge us for our food.

The black men and women have shown that eating out—one of the favorite pastimes of blacks and whites—is a worrisome expe-rience to black Americans. Restaurant owners can change this behavior. They can manifest integrity and dignity by treating all diners the same and by requiring all their employees to implement the same attitude, thereby giving all their customers a pleasant dining-out experience.

Another place where students face racism is at public swimming pools, even decades after desegregation. And no matter where in the country these encounters occurred, they all followed the same pattern. Sometimes the students reported having bad experiences at pools when they were too young to understand what was occurring. At other times, they felt inferior, hurt, and angry.

Blacks often live in neighborhoods where there are no swimming pools, and the only way they can swim is go to a pool in a white neighborhood. In Robert's case, even the pool down the street from his house in Tennessee presented problems. This twenty-one-year-old college student told me:

> When I was about ten years old, a couple of friends and I wanted to swim. There was a pool down the street from my house where we went to swim. Everyone there was white. I should've known, but at the age of ten, you don't think about those things. The man came to the fence and told us that we couldn't come in because we were not members. I said that all we wanted to do was swim. He said, "I told you that you can't come in." I asked, "How can we become members?" He said, "They aren't taking new members." I asked, "When do you plan to take in new members?" Then he said, "Look, I said that you can't come in, so get your little black ass out of here." We went home.
>
> When my father came home from work, I told him what the white man had said. My mother told him to call the police, because she didn't want my father to visit the man himself and get in trouble. The police went to the pool, and the man denied that he had said those things to us. I was hurt for three reasons. First of all, I was hurt because at the age of ten, I was self-con-

scious about being dark-skinned. Second, I was hurt because the man didn't let us swim. Third, I had never been called "black" by a white person. I just couldn't understand. This swimming pool was located in an all-black neighborhood. There wasn't a white family within a square mile of my house. Yet they used the pool and denied us the opportunity to swim.

George, twenty-six and a Virginia resident, echoed Robert's experience:

When I was fifteen years old I visited a cousin in Nashville, North Carolina, in 1983. We decided to go swimming. When we got to the swimming pool, there was a sign posted that read: "For Members only and Their Guests." My cousin continued walking toward the pool, and the people started yelling, "Y'all can't come in here. This pool is for members only and their guests." How did they know that we weren't members? My cousin believed that the reason we were not allowed to swim was because we are black. Because we couldn't get in, my cousin was embarrassed. He was already dressed for swimming. He told me, "There's nothing that I can do. Let's go home." So we left.

As we have seen, George's cousin's conclusion, "There is nothing that I can do," was a common theme in the students' stories about their experiences with racism, as was needing to leave the "scene of the crime."

Christopher, twenty-five and from Ohio, described being made to feel like a pariah while at the pool:

As a young kid of about ten years old, I went to my cousin's house in northern Chicago, where the community was mostly white and upper class. One day we went swimming in the community pool. While we swam, we noticed that we were the only two blacks there, and that all the white kids had started getting out of the pool. After a while, we noticed that our clothes and towels were gone. The white kids had hidden them and were throwing them around. Because we felt insulted, my cousin and I got out of the pool and ran home, crying all the way. We thought that we had done something wrong, until my uncle explained the situation and told us not to worry, because he would build a swimming pool in his backyard. We were happy that we would never have to return to that pool. It also made me feel how cruel white people can really be.

Going to resorts can be a wonderful experience. Staying in lovely hotels on ocean fronts, walking on beaches, playing in the tides, riding in elevators barefooted and in bathing suits, swimming and playing in the ocean are what blacks enjoy—just like whites.

Most older blacks do not patronize resort areas that aren't accustomed to black clientele and therefore don't provide a pleasurable experience. One summer my husband and I were pushed for time. So we decided to take a two-week vacation in a state bordering Virginia, where we live. We spent a handsome sum of money for our room. But before we could get a room that was comparable to the cost, we had to change it three times. Our vacation was ruined before we even got settled. We should have left, but we needed a rest. The unpleasant expressions on the faces of the people at the lobby desk were another spoiler. Worst of all, we were forced to contend with the most unprofessional maître d's we had ever encountered. We ate all our meals at the hotel. At first they seated us in a favorable section of the restaurant—sections that had chairs with cushions or by windows with an ocean view. Later we were seated in corners and near servers' stations. The wait staff gave poor service that ruined most of our meals. An elderly black male employee had observed the misery of our expensive vacation. In private, he advised us not to return. He told us that the resort had only a small black clientele and that they didn't care for blacks. The resort area is near us, and we'd love to spend a few days there from time to time, but at the beginning of 2000 we know better. It is time for resort owners to extend goodwill to all their clients. They should understand that racism at their resorts makes blacks pay for whites to mistreat them, and it deprives and angers people who seek rest and enjoyment.

Young blacks rarely think of the consequences of going to resorts with small black clienteles. Consequently, the college students also experienced racism on vacation at resorts. They often had difficulty obtaining rooms. Once they overcame that hurdle, they were often followed by hotel personnel. Kwabyna, from Washington, D.C., described her experience:

> I'm not even twenty years old, but I've had terrible experiences with racism. For example, friends and I stayed at a hotel in a Virginia resort city. It was definitely nice and expensive. Because we were black, they acted as though they didn't want to rent us a room. After assigning the room, they listened through the door to see how many people were in the room. While staying in the hotel, we visited nearby shops and stores on the oceanfront. The salespeople followed us around and asked repeatedly, "Do you need help?" Needless to say, our oceanfront visit was not a happy experience.

Kwabyna and her friends had chosen a resort unaccustomed to serving blacks. Unfortunately, they didn't know that resorts without a history of accepting blacks will not be accommodating—to say the least.

The young people in my study also made it clear that racism at hotels—from five-star luxury hotels to much cheaper accommodations—is rampant. The trouble begins as soon as a black person arrives at the registration desk. Often hotel clerks deny that any rooms are available without reservations. Yet even when the room has been reserved, it is most often beneath the fifth floor in a high-rise hotel, when in actuality, the best rooms in large hotels start at about the eighth floor. And black students report that their preference was often disregarded when their rooms were assigned to them.

Melvin, twenty-three, related this experience at Virginia Beach, the world's largest resort town:

At my job in Delaware, I met and became friends with Calvin, who is white. Calvin heard me talking about going to Virginia Beach, Virginia, for a weekend of fun. Two other black guys were also going. Calvin wanted to go and agreed to help share the expenses. My two other friends agreed that it was all right for Calvin to go. They had met him through me and found him to be a down-to-earth white guy.

The weekend trip finally took place. We arrived in Virginia Beach at three o'clock one Friday afternoon. The weather was great—a hot ninety degrees. We drove down the strip checking out the scene and the girls. Then we decided to check into a hotel. We carefully selected one that we had observed had the most beautiful girls. I wanted to be impressive, so I got out of the car and went to talk to the hotel clerk to get a room, while Calvin, Mitchell, and Keith took the luggage out of the car. I entered the lobby of the hotel, and a middle-aged white man stood behind the check-in desk. While I was approaching the desk, with wallet in hand, the desk clerk immediately said, "No vacancies." I became somewhat puzzled. I wondered whether he was talking to me or someone else. I proceeded to the desk and told him that I would like a room. The clerk this time rudely stated: "I said that we have no vacancies." I responded by saying that the sign outside said that there were vacancies. He informed me that the last room had become occupied a minute earlier.

Angrily, I walked out of the hotel. I informed the guys what had happened. One of my two black friends suggested that we leave and go to another hotel. However, the sign outside the hotel never changed. Calvin became somewhat irate and said, "Let me try." With his surfboard under his arm, he walked into the lobby, smiling. Then he walked up to the desk clerk and requested a room with double beds. He gave the clerk the requested identification and money and was issued a room.

Once Calvin was given the key, he smiled and yelled, "Yo, home boys, come on in. We're in the house." As we entered the lobby, I was the first black face the hotel clerk saw. While all four of us walked by the front desk, I watched for reactions. The desk clerk's face was red. I walked by and said, "Hey guys, you think we just rented the last room?" Then I smiled and took the elevator to the fifth floor, where our room was located.

Melvin and Calvin are not rare. Well-intentioned whites have been "fronting" for blacks for years. In this case, Calvin's actions showed up the racist hotel clerk, and the group of friends went on to enjoy a fun-filled weekend.

Movie theaters can also prove to be daunting places for blacks. Fred, from Virginia, described what happened when he and his friends went to see *Boyz 'n the Hood*. Many whites like to see movies about blacks. So ticket sellers save the tickets for whites. When Fred and his friends reached the ticket booth, the white cashier told them the movie was sold out. As they walked away, a group of white boys asked for and were sold tickets to the same movie. Fred and his friends went back to the ticket booth and asked the cashier why he had let the white kids in after he had told them the movie was sold out. Out of frustration, Fred told him, "Every time a movie dealing with blacks comes to this theater, something bad always happens. It is caused by too many of you watching black movies." Because so many films are filled with white characters, it is refreshing for young blacks to see movies with predominantly black characters. Yet all too often, white viewers are given precedence and blacks are kept from seeing the movies when they want to.

Donald, twenty-two and from Michigan, was standing outside a theater with his white girlfriend in Hampton, Virginia. Suddenly, he sensed someone staring at him. Glancing up, he saw an older white couple looking down their noses at them. They began pointing and saying, loud enough for others to hear, "Interracial relations are wrong." Donald became uncomfortable with his girlfriend as well as embarrassed and angry. "But there was nothing that I could do, so I broke up with the lady," he said. Regardless of the hurt it causes, all too often blacks have little recourse against racism.

Even in places where blacks and whites should be able to peacefully enjoy their shared history in the United States, blacks suffer from racism. Barbara, eighteen and from Virginia, recounted this story about her family vacation:

> We went to Natural Bridge, Virginia, for our family vacation. Upon entering the town, we noticed that we were the only blacks. Strange looks came from everywhere. They seemed to say, with their eyes, that we weren't welcome.
>
> When we ran out of snacks, we went to a store in town. At the same time that we approached the counter, a white man also arrived. Although we were at the counter first, the white clerk wanted to serve him first instead. It was right for us to receive service first. We were required to pay the bill before receiving our food.
>
> In the same town, my family and I went to a swimming pool. We noticed that we were the only ones in the pool. Whites walked up to the pool and looked at us. Then they either left the pool or waited until we had gotten out. I had never experienced racism like this and was deeply upset. Yet I'm not even twenty-one years old.

The students in my study also spoke of encountering racism at public areas such as parks. Underlying most of their experiences was white people's perception that whites should always come first. Melissa gave the following account:

> One summer my cousins and I went to a park in Florida. While there, I went to a water fountain. It just so happened that an elderly white woman arrived after me. She gave me the evil eye. It seemed to say that she was supposed to go first. I said to her, "Slavery days are over." She grunted and walked away. Nothing else happened. I simply continued drinking and left the fountain. However, I asked myself the question, "Did she really expect me to stop drinking water and let her drink?" Perhaps the way things used to be were etched in her mind. That is, "separate water fountains."

The days of separate water fountains, which provided blacks with warm water to drink and whites with cold water, have long since disappeared. But the mentality hasn't; apparently, it has just gone in a new direction. That is, blacks should step back and let whites drink first.

The most difficult places to go turned out to be just about everywhere, including automobile dealers. There is little that is more fun to young people than buying a car—especially their first. But so many white salespeople make buying a car for recreation and personal needs a regretful experience. Often when a black potential buyer drives up, white salespeople stand around a few minutes before offering help. The same is true when black customers enter the showroom. Salespersons at car dealers suffer from a virus that cripples prospective black car buyers. They are determined to select cheap cars for blacks and prevent them from buying comfortable cars. White salesmen aggressively attempt to spend blacks' money the way they want to spend it.

When the young black students whom I interviewed attempted to purchase cars, they reported encountering all kinds of problems, such as hiked prices, shoddy service, and poor interpersonal rela-

tions. For example, when Glenn was twenty-two years old, he purchased a car from a local car dealer in Norfolk, Virginia. After
Glenn bought the car, the salesman increased the price, and Glenn
paid the additional amount. Subsequently, on several occasions
when Glenn brought in his car for repairs, the people there were
rude to him. After those ordeals, Glenn stated, "My feelings toward
white people is that they are devils. Although I believe there are
some good white people, I choose not to deal with them all
together, because I feel that, on a whole, they are a wicked race. I
feel that we should separate from them, because they are only using
blacks." Jacking up the price for black customers—who are looking
for everything from houses to cars—is unfortunately a widespread
practice and no secret among blacks, who are painfully aware that
they are being asked to pay more simply because of their skin color.

Glenn was not alone in having difficulty purchasing a car.
When Delbridge, twenty-eight and from Delaware, was twenty, this
is what happened to him:

> During the summer of 1987, I went to the local Jenson deal-
> ership to price a new Mustang Grand Touring (GT). After I
> had been walking around on the lot for several minutes, not
> one salesman approached me, but I could see three or four of
> them being idle and looking out the showroom window at me.
> I would hate to guess what they were thinking.
>
> Finally, one of them came out. I told him that I was inter-
> ested in the Mustang GT. He gave me the information about
> the car that I wanted. I went home and discussed it with my
> parents. About two days later, I returned with my father,
> because we were going to purchase the car. The salesman who
> had waited on me before was busy. Someone else came out
> to assist us.
>
> I'll never forget him or his name. He approached us as if
> we were a joke. He said, "What can I do for you fellas?" I told
> him the car that I was interested in, that I had talked with his

co-worker about it, and that I was serious about purchasing it. Immediately he told me the price, which I already knew. Then he asked me, "Where do you work?" I told him that I worked at a local hospital, and then he asked, "In housekeeping or the kitchen?" My father began to frown. Before I could tell him that I was a college student studying physical therapy, my father told him that he should watch how he talks to customers. Then the salesman said, "No offense, but your son should really look at the Escort GT. It is less expensive."

Delbridge's story was sadly very similar to those told by most of the young black men who attempted to buy a new car. In these stories we can see some familiar racist stereotypes rearing their ugly heads: that if you're young and black you can't afford anything nice and moreover, you don't deserve to be treated with the respect shown to your white peers. Black America calls upon all car dealerships to end racism on their lots and in their showrooms.

Health Clubs

Young blacks, like the whites they see at health clubs, enjoy working out. Black men and women have begun to take aerobic classes, walk on the track at health clubs, lift weights, swim, enjoy the steam room and sauna, and exercise on the countless mobile machines. They want to lose weight, enhance their strength, get in shape, exercise, or just relax. Yet their enjoyment is marred by racism. The white men and women at the desk are the first obstacle. They often practice racism before any exercise even takes place. Some desk employees simply won't speak to blacks. If they do speak, they don't usually tell them to have a good workout like they tell whites. Of course there are exceptions, but too many people fall into the racist category. My black friends who have had unpleasant encounters at health clubs simply made up their minds to discount ignorant employees and fellow club members and get on with their exercise. Fortunately, health clubs are changing. Some hire black men and women to teach aerobics classes. It's not unusual to see blacks and whites exercising together. I have both black and white friends at my health club, and we enjoy good friendship and conversation. Yet health clubs still have a long way to go. Eric, twenty-two and a Virginia resident, had this difficult experience:

> Early this summer [1993], I was working out at a health club in Hampton, Virginia. After finishing my workout, I went to the locker room to take a shower and dress for work. While I was in the shower, three white guys came in and began staring at me. One of them said, "You look like Buck Wheat." I was sort of shocked by this whole ordeal. I asked him what he had said. He repeated himself. That's when all of his friends began laughing. I didn't think that the situation was amusing. I started toward the guy. Before I could get to him, my friend grabbed me. I was so frustrated by this whole incident that I went straight home and missed work that day. I couldn't believe that this had happened. I haven't been to that gym since.

Eric had such a heart-wrenching experience that he ended up missing a day of work—something he rarely did.

WALKING AND OTHER MEANS OF TRANSPORTATION

The young men and women spoke of encountering racist behavior at other public areas such as on sidewalks. This kind of behavior underscores the broad scope of racism. Nobody, black or white, can do without sidewalks. Practicing racism in a setting where freedom should be taken for granted should cause angst in the heart of every white American. The students told me many stories about painful encounters they had on sidewalks. This type of racism also has its historical roots. Blacks have passed down, from generation to generation, slave stories having to do with city sidewalks. One story is that, during slave times, when blacks met whites on city sidewalks, blacks had to step off until the whites passed. Another frequently handed-down story is that when blacks wanted to laugh while walking down city sidewalks, they had to go to the corner and put their heads in special laughing boxes constructed by whites.

The students in my study recounted modern-day versions of these stories. While Frederic, a twenty-one-year-old Ohio resident, and his friends were venturing down a Virginia street, the sidewalk narrowed. When they arrived at that end of the sidewalk, they met a young white couple coming toward them from the opposite direction. They slowed down to make room for the couple. The young woman grasped her male friend's arm tightly, and the couple proceeded to walk faster with their backs hunched, while saying "excuse me" an excessive number of times. Frederic and his two friends turned to one another and laughed. According to Frederic, "The fear of the unknown in their eyes was too funny for words." Although Frederic and his friends had treated the couple courteously, the couple still overreacted out of their fear of having to share the same pavement with young black men.

Ronald's experience was more blatant: One pleasant afternoon in 1991, Ronald, twenty-three and from Virginia, was walking downtown in Norfolk, Virginia. He was trying to clear his head, wanting only to be alone. A white man came toward him from the opposite direction. Ronald kept walking. When the white man got close to him, he said, "Walk in the street because sidewalks are for white people and white people only." Although Ronald didn't move, he looked at the man as if he were crazy. He started to respond, then changed his mind. Ronald's case is typical of how the young people sometimes felt. They wanted to say or do something in response to racism but weren't sure that anything would be effective. How incredible that in the 1990s a young black man could be told that sidewalks were only for whites—something not even the slaves were told.

And again, like everywhere else, many of the young people were treated to racial slurs while out walking. Christine, twenty-one and from Connecticut, related that when she was a teenager, she and her cousin were walking down a street. A white man pushed her slightly and called her a "nigger bitch." Similarly, Natika, twenty years old and living in D.C., related that once when she and her friends were walking to the basketball court, on the way, some whites called them niggers. Sometimes racial slurs were combined with other types of harassment. Monica related this example:

> In the ninth grade, I was walking down the sidewalk one day. A white man drove his car beside me, proceeded to call me nigger, and threw a soda bottle at me. The contents ruined my new white dress. I was scared and angry. I went home and told my brother. My brother ran after him, but didn't find him. Later I thought about this incident and was angry for a long time. In the meantime, my mother tried to convince me that not all white people are bad.

How tragic that a young girl couldn't even walk down the street without having to be robbed of her innocence so unexpectedly. And what a trial for her mother, who had the difficult task of convincing her daughter that she shouldn't lose trust of all white people.

Rest stops are placed conveniently along our highways for the millions of Americans who like driving to their destinations. There weary travelers can relax, use the restrooms, and maybe eat a snack. Yet even at rest stops many blacks can't take a break from racism. Eric related a story of how young children faced racism when they were traveling with members of their church:

> It is hard to recollect all the exact details about this experience, because it happened years ago. But the event itself is still fresh in my head. My friend Ronnie and I were on our way to Niagara Falls with the church we attended. We were between the ages of twelve and fourteen years. Ronnie has darker skin than me. It really didn't mean anything to me

then, and it still doesn't. However, I soon learned what it means in the eyes of whites.

The bus driver pulled into the rest area. Ronnie and I were the first ones to get off the bus. Upon entering the restroom, we were the only two persons in there with one white maintenance man. I don't know what happened word for word, but it went something like this. The white man said, "What kind of trouble are you boys about to get into?"

We just looked at each other, wondering what he was talking about. I proceeded to ask him. The maintenance man said with a funny grin, "I'm not worried about you, but I'm worried about your friend." Ronnie asked, "What do you mean by that?" By that time, our church members began entering the restroom, and the maintenance man slipped out.

Ronnie and I kind of shook it off, but it still stays in my head until this day. That bad feeling became the most memorable part of my church trip.

As Eric thought about his experience, he realized that his skin color gave him an advantage over his darker-skinned friend. Now a college student, Ronnie knows what adult blacks know. Since whites often suspect rightly that light-skinned blacks are the products of black-white relationships, they accord these lighter-skinned blacks more respect.

Public transportation is another arena in which racism is rampant. Subways proved to be particularly troublesome places for many young blacks. On one occasion Reginald, twenty, got on the subway in New York and proceeded to his seat. When he was getting ready to sit down, a white woman clenched her purse, got up, and said, "I would rather not sit down." Letitia, also twenty and from Pennsylvania, had a similar experience:

I was approaching the gate to the subway station in Philadelphia, Pennsylvania, after work. I was anxious to get

home and relax. That particular day at work had been stress-
ful. When the subway door opened, and the exiting
passengers were leaving the train, I was the first person to
get on the train. I preferred sitting alone, but there was no
single seat available. I walked toward the back of the train.
That section, too, was full. Unable to find a seat alone, I sat
beside a white woman. When I sat down, she moved over. I
was minding my own business. Yet she grabbed her purse. I
was offended. She clenched it in a manner that suggested
I was about to hold her up in a full subway train. Consequently, I sat on the edge of my seat; I was pissed off and
looked for another seat. None was available. When the train
came to another stop, the white woman remained in the seat,
but I abruptly moved elsewhere. My stop was approaching.
When I got up to get off the train, I looked at her and rolled
my eyes. Even though it was a wrong gesture on my part, at
the time, I felt it was appropriate. I don't think about it as
much as I used to. However, I am thankful that all white
people are not like that woman.

Many other young blacks I spoke with had similar stories to tell
about white people clenching their purses or changing their seats
on the subway.

Often college students also encountered racism on city buses.
Cashawn, nineteen and from Virginia, described her 1993 experience:

While I was riding the bus to work, a boarding passenger, a
white female, noted that the majority of the passengers seated
in front of the bus were black. She then made this racist comment, "They should all be seated in the back of the bus where
they belong."

Other passengers and I sat in shock with our mouths
hung open. I couldn't believe that in today's society such a
comment could be made. A seated black passenger, angered

by the woman's comment, asked her, "Have you ever heard of Mrs. Rosa Parks?" She answered, "Yes," and wanted to know why she was questioned. The passenger replied, "Because of Mrs. Parks, we're able to sit anywhere we damn well please on this bus." The remainder of the passengers cheered him. The older white woman remained standing on the bus until she was able to sit alone.

Even though she was old, I didn't feel sorry for her. She chose to stand. Inside I was hoping that she would stand until we arrived at her stop. I also laughed to myself, as she swayed from side to side and occasionally stumbled while the driver turned street corners and continued his route. This reaction helped my anger to subside.

In some ways the bus experience in the 1990s is as vivid as Rosa Parks's experience was in the 1960s. Sadly, some whites still believe that blacks should stand or sit in the back; they believe that whites still come first. But young people can tell themselves, when they are harassed by racists, that Rosa Parks, Martin Luther King Jr., and throngs of unknown black Americans earned them the right to sit any place they choose.

Sometimes it can be no easier to ride in a taxi than to ride on a subway or in a bus. Bruce, twenty and from New York, related this 1994 experience:

In Virginia, my girlfriend and I took a cab from a movie theater to the dormitory, and the driver attempted to take us the wrong route. He was a tall white man with brown hair. When we discovered that he was taking us the wrong way, we jumped out of the taxi and ran. He started looking for us. He didn't find us, because we were hiding. When he drove away, we knocked on people's doors for help, but no one came to their door. Finally, a white man came out of his house and said that he didn't have a telephone. By this time, we were scared and started yelling,

"Please help us." He told us to get away from his house or he would call the police. At first, he didn't have a telephone. All of a sudden, he had one. He began calling us names. For example, he said, "Niggers, get out of this area quick. You don't belong here." We discovered that the taxi driver had taken us to a racist neighborhood. A white lady called the police, and they came. We told the officers what had happened. They took us to the university. We described the taxi driver's appearance and identified his cab company. The police caught him, and we took him to court. The judge only fined him for failure to take us to our right destination.

I was hurt over the incident. While trying to get out of the white neighborhood, I received a bad cut from climbing gates and contracted a terrible headache from crying. This is the most horrible thing that has ever happened to me with white people.

Young blacks reported that being taken the long way to run up the fare was a common occurrence for them. In this case the driver took Gene and his girlfriend to a place where they would feel especially uncomfortable. And even though they got out of the taxi driver's clutches, they weren't able to escape the racism in the neighborhood.

FARM LIFE

Slavery and most sharecropping no longer exist. However, there are still pockets of poor black farm workers throughout the South. They need somebody to speak for them. Their wages are low, and their living conditions are deplorable. Though white landowners see the conditions of their farm families, they still practice the racism of denying farmers fair treatment. Kenneth, twenty-three and a resident of North Carolina, described this experience on a farm:

I was sixteen years old. Every summer I visited my grand-mother in Emporia, Virginia, and helped a white man in his fields. The man always picked me up in the morning and returned me home in the afternoon.

One day, we were working in the field together. While I was bending over, he swung his hoe and hit my butt. He just looked at me and said, "Oh, you're strong. You'll be okay." He never let me stop working. Later that day he made me sit in the back of his dirty truck and ride home.

My mother ended up taking me to the emergency room. They put four stitches in my buttock. The white man never told my mother what had happened. I told my sister and she had told Mama. My mother took him to court that forced him to pay the medical bills.

At that time, I didn't think of him as a racist. I thought that it was my fault. When I became older and understood racism better, I was angry with myself.

Although some of the students in this book recognized racism at a young age, others did not, as in Kenneth's case. As we have seen from the stories in these chapters, racism occurs everywhere, from farms to Wall Street, from North to South, and from East to West. It is here, there, and everywhere.

WHAT TO DO ABOUT IT

Blacks know all too well how racist acts can spoil such events as eating out or working out. Many white people are unfortunately rude, insulting, and demeaning to the blacks they encounter in these places. What black Americans want most is to enjoy the same ease and comfort that white Americans take for granted, whether they're in a restaurant, at a movie theater, at a car dealer, or on a city sidewalk.

What White People Can Do

For the purposes of brevity, let us concentrate on restaurants and hotels in this discussion, leaving the reader to extrapolate how what happens in these settings can be applied to other situations. A maître d' (literally, "master of the house") or concierge (literally "fellow servant") is typically the first person a patron encounters at a restaurant or hotel. This person, therefore, should ensure that all patrons are treated with respect and dignity. People, black and white, go to these places to have fun, to relax, and to be entertained. Maybe they've gone to meet friends or conduct business or to celebrate some family occasion.

People should be seated in the order in which they arrive or make reservations, regardless of their skin color. And everyone should be offered the best seats or rooms available at the time. Waiters and other servers should treat all patrons with respectful friendliness. Service should be prompt and willing.

As any restaurant patron knows, all it takes is bad service to ruin an otherwise wonderful meal. Black people shouldn't be rushed more than any other customers or made to feel unwelcome in any way. Special requests—sending back an entrée, asking for extra dishes, and so forth—should be met with the same cheerful willingness that any white person would receive.

Making eye contact with patrons is always important. Little touches can go a long way. Simple gestures like saying "Thanks for coming" or "We hope that you come back again, soon" can be powerful, especially to a black American who has experienced rejection and rudeness so many times before. And it goes without saying—or it should—that the same price should be charged to everyone, regardless of race.

One does not need to be a concierge or maître d' to work on eliminating racist behaviors. Whenever a black person is receiving poor service, white patrons need to register their objections to such behavior, either with the server directly or with the manager (or both). Especially effective is communicating that one only eats (lodges, sees movies, buys cars, and so forth) at establishments that treat all clients graciously and equally. Then enforce such a policy.

Also helpful and appreciated are appropriate acknowledgments from white guests. Looking black patrons in the eyes and saying, "Good evening" or "How are you this evening?" for example, can signal your acceptance of a peer.

What Black People Can Do

Black people can practice being good restaurant and hotel patrons so that those establishments have every reason to want to welcome them back. Such patrons dress appropriately for their destination. They speak in moderate voices and don't disturb fellow diners or guests. They are patient when serving staff gets behind on busy nights. And these ideal patrons treat their servers as human beings, with the same respect and dignity they want for themselves. When service is good, they tip well. They say thank you and compliment the chef or owner.

CONCLUSION

I had seven purposes in writing this book. It is my hope that the first, and the most vital, to create greater awareness of racism among whites, has been achieved. The stories we have read make it abundantly clear that racism hurts and angers young people and prevents their progress—and so much more. It is my belief and my hope that my white readers will take these young people seriously and will strive to have the integrity and dignity not to cause more hurt to black Americans. Second, as a result of whites treating blacks better, I believe that all relations between blacks and whites can be improved. Good black-white relations are both personally and socially satisfying.

Third, scholars like Oscar Lewis and Julius Wilson have focused solely on the underclass. In my opinion, if scholars draw grand conclusions, they must prove that what they say is true about all black social classes. My students and I did just that. After talking with the young students, I drew the conclusion that economic status is not necessarily perpetuating, and that racism gets in black people's way far more than social class does. Without racism, even blacks living in the worst pockets of poverty in the great American cities could break free, get an education, find good jobs with appropriate raises and promotions, and enjoy life away from their jobs.

My fourth reason for writing *Everyday Racism* was that for a long time, I have been bothered by Professor Gunnar Myrdal's *An American Dilemma*. The content of this classic is negative, which was necessary to prove that blacks are a problem for whites. But mostly I was disturbed about his conclusion in which he indicates that racism disturbs the American heart. I think my students' stories have shown that the agony is in the hearts of *black* Americans.

Fifth, I was not interested in talking about slavery. Instead, I wanted an update on modern race relations. Young blacks and black adults are more concerned with their lives today than they are about slavery. I found that black-white relations are riddled with racism even today, and I became weary of reading about its style and settings, but no solutions or pleas for it to end. No mention of the hurt. No mention of calling for all white Americans to work toward eradicating racism. With this book, filled mostly with racist stories from the 1990s, I am calling for precisely that.

The specific effects of racism on black people have long concerned me. As I thought back over my twenty-five years of social research and scanned the American landscape from the North to the South and the East to the West, I saw and experienced racism. It often begins in innocent young white children's lives and lasts a lifetime; blacks face it from infancy to death. I wanted to uncover this awful human dynamic and to explore what it actually does in the lives of real black people. I am calling on every white person in America to cleanse themselves of the racist malady that causes blacks to suffer so greatly.

Finally, Professor Myrdal encouraged me, as much as anything else, to give an insider's view. I don't actually mind that he was a

Swedish economist. One of my best research experiences was as an outsider in Osuwem, Ghana, West Africa. However, I know that it was difficult for Professor Myrdal to do justice to the dilemma of blacks. First, he was commissioned to write his book in 1944 by an American corporation. That alone tied his hands. Instead of talking to blacks in this country, he talked with whites and used their research. In effect, he was asking whites to give him the answer to their own wrongdoing. That was too much for me to bare. I knew racism as a sharecropper. I knew it during segregation, and I've known it since segregation. I knew that my perspective, and that of my students, was needed to shed valuable light on the specter of racism.

Racism is a huge problem in this country that needs to be countered. I can't do it alone. I need the help of all white America. Gradual eradication is not enough. Racism has already damaged too many generations. White Americans, we black Americans need you to cure yourselves of the racist virus once and for all. You have the power to do it. You have the integrity, morality, and uprightness. We *can* have a country with freedom for all. A country that will influence the rest of the world in a greater way than we have ever known in the area of human rights. At long last, the people who descended from the folks who appeared in advertisements like this one across the South will enjoy life. Although this advertisement appeared in *Atlanta Intelligencer* in 1864, it still serves to encapsulate the sentiments still held by too many. It should serve as a clarion call to end white racism forever.

> Robert A. Crawford
> (Formerly Crawford, Frazer & Co.)
> NEGRO DEALER
> Peachtree Street, Atlanta, Georgia
> The most expensive Negro depot in the Confederacy,
> clean, healthy, safe, and comfortable.
> Porters experienced and trusty lock-up
> Discipline and fare, all right.

STOCK CONSTANTLY REPLENISHED
usually on hand
cooks (meat and pastry), washers, and ironers,
house servants, and seamstresses, blacksmiths,
carpenters, field hands, shoemakers,
plow boys and girls, body servants, waiters,
drivers and families,
My extensive acquaintance and long experience in
the business secure speedy and satisfactory sales.
Parties sending me Negroes by railroad will find
my old and trusty porters, Andrew and
Anthony, about the train as usual.[1]

Like whites, blacks have made great contributions to this country. We need the people who sit idly by and the perpetrators of racism to free black Americans. Not only did their ancestors help build America, but they have put their own mark on this country through hard labor and subservience. It is my greatest hope that all white Americans will open their hearts and minds to practice fairness, kindness, and graciousness everywhere they go, with everyone they meet. I have shared these stories about racism to help bring whites and blacks together—to care for each other and to treat each other with respect and dignity. That's justice. That's American. I know that white America can change. I can't wait for the very minute when whites ring out racism and ring in black freedom, justice, and respect, the same way that we rang in the twenty-first century. I can see you now ringing those liberty bells for black American freedom. My gratitude.

NOTES

INTRODUCTION: I'M BLACK AND I'M PROUD

1. Oscar Lewis, *The Five Families* (New York: Basic Books, 1965), xliii–xliv; William Julius Wilson, *The Declining Significance of Race* (Chicago: University of Chicago Press, 1978), ix.

2. Joe R. Feagin and Clairece Booher Feagin, *Discrimination American Style: Institutional Racism and Sexism* (Englewood Cliffs, N.J.: Prentice-Hall, 1978).

3. Gunnar Myrdal, *An American Dilemma* (New Brunswick, Can.: Transaction Publishers, 1996), lxxix. Myrdal held the same view in 1996 as he held in the book's first edition in 1944.

1. WHEN IT HAPPENS NEXT DOOR

1. Franklin M. Garrett, *Atlanta and Its Environs*, vol. 1 (New York: Lewis Historical Publishing, 1954), 61.

2. Marvin Harris, "Race Relations Research: Auspices and Results in the United States," *Social Science Information* 1 (1962): 28–51.

3. White racist military men peddled this same type of racism on the Pacific Islands during World War II, when the military was segregated. The white troops arrived on the Pacific Islands first. When they got there they told the young island women that the blacks troops were coming and that the women should be on guard because they had tails. Later Mr. Boone's black battalion arrived. Mr. Boone went courting one night. The young woman he was with asked him if he had a tail. He said, "Yes," and asked, "Would you like to see it?" She said, "Yes." Needless

to say, they had a fine night of fun and lovemaking. She learned that black "tails" are just like white tails.

2. FROM DAY CARE TO GRADUATE SCHOOL

1. Carter G. Woodson, *The Education of the Negro Prior to 1861* (Washington, D.C.: Associated Publishers, 1919), 228.

2. Woodson, *Education of the Negro,* 206, 208.

3. August Meier and Elliott Rudwick, *From Plantation to Ghetto,* 3d ed. (New York: Hill and Wang, 1966), 74.

4. Woodson, *Education of the Negro,* 218.

5. Denise Watson Batts, *The Virginian-Pilot,* December 5, 1999.

6. Annie Barnes, *Retention of African-American Males in High School* (Lanham, Md.: University Press of America, 1992), 79–80.

7. Barnes, *Retention of African-American Males,* 71.

8. Betty Murphy, "From Janitor to Manager," *Opportunity* (1971): 30, 32.

9. Barnes, *Retention of African-American Males,* 56.

3. AT THE STORE

1. Although the research for this book did not extend to the experience of middle-age black women, I know a woman who asked to try on a $600 dress. The white saleswoman told her that it was not their custom to allow black women to try on dresses that cost more than $300. The woman indicated that she was planning, in fact, to purchase the more expensive dress, if she were first given the chance to try it on to ensure that it fit properly. Such unequal treatment drastically cuts down on a black person's pleasure in shopping for luxury items. Moreover, stores with racist sales staff are losing present and future sales.

2. This case is particularly tragic. The black man did not want to search the young woman. But he felt he had to because his white supervisor had told him to. Perhaps it was the only way he could keep his job. So many blacks in authority in schools, businesses, and even churches hurt other blacks to maintain favor with their white superiors. This is as true in the church as elsewhere. Blacks in white churches fervently and tearfully extol the white members' purity concerning race. They claim that their lovely churches are free of racism. For almost thirty years, I have had close association with white churches and black churches. I am truly an expert in the ways of congregations of both races, and I have yet to find one free of racism.

My years of intimacy with congregations of both races lead me to conclude that no one can state accurately that racism does not exist in his or her church. They simply don't know what other members are experiencing. My experience has proven that church members are at risk to even vouch for the Christianity of even one church member. Believe me, many white Christians and many black Christians commit sin while implementing their Christian duties. There is no pure church—white or black—interracially or Christianly. This doesn't mean there aren't exceptions. It does mean that they are few. If they exist, it would be wonderful if they would rise up and be models for churchgoing America. I fervently love good racial and interracial relations and high morality or Christianity.

Whites using blacks to mistreat other blacks is nothing new. In slave times, white people used black overseers to keep other blacks in line. What is surprising is that nearly two hundred years later whites are still using blacks to punish their own people.

4. IN THE WORKPLACE

1. Lynn Walker, "On Employment Discrimination," *Essence* 4 (1973): 24; Joe R. Feagin and Clairece Booher Feagin, *Discrimination American Style: Institutional Racism and Sexism* (Englewood Cliffs, N.J.: Prentice-Hall, 1978), 58.

2. Frances M. Beal, "Slave of a Slave No More: Black Women in Struggle," *The Black Scholar* (1975): 7; Shirley Chisholm, "Racism and Anti-Feminism," *The Black Scholar* (1970): 41; Elizabeth Hood, "Black Women, White Women: Separate Paths to Liberation," *The Black Scholar* (1978): 46.

3. Gary Becker, *The Economics of Discrimination* (Chicago: University of Chicago Press, 1957), 3, 6; Herbert Hill, "Postponement of Economic Equality," *The Black Scholar* (1977): 18.

4. Annie Barnes, *Black Women: Interpersonal Relationships in Profile* (Bristol: Wyndam Hall Press, 1986), 34.

5. Marsha's case is actually more complicated than reported. Marsha's employer made a number of sexual advances toward Marsha and another black female employee. They told his wife about his sexual advances. All he did was give them one week of unpaid vacation. It became impossible to continue a working relationship.

5. BLACKS AND LAW ENFORCEMENT

1. Annie Barnes, "Comparative Study of Policing in America," *Droit et cultures* 33 (1997): 108.

6. FROM EATING OUT TO WORKING OUT

1. Franklin M. Garrett, *Atlanta and Its Environs*, vol. 1 (New York: Lewis Historical Publishing, 1954), 61.